ML
410
F219
A3

Fanshawe, David
African sanctus

**DATE DUE**

| DEC 3 '75 | | | |
|---|---|---|---|
| MAY 12 76 | | | |
| | | | |
| | | | |
| | | | |
| | | | |
| | | | |
| | | | |
| | | | |
| | | | |
| | | | |
| | | | |
| | | | |

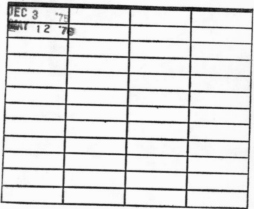

'AFRICAN SANCTUS'

# AFRICAN SANCTUS

*A Story of Travel and Music*

David Fanshawe

# AFRICAN SANCTUS

*A Story of Travel and Music*

Quadrangle/The New York Times Book Co.

I long for the belly of Africa, I long for the
stampede in the elephant grass – the native
dances – the throb of hearts burnt by the sons of
Blue Mountains.

*African Sanctus*, Chapter VII

The extract from 'The Parable of the Old Man and
the Young' by Wilfred Owen is quoted by permission
of Chatto & Windus Ltd and New Directions
Publishing Corporation
© Chatto & Windus Ltd 1946, 1963

Library of Congress Cataloging in Publication Data

Fanshawe, David, 1942
    African Sanctus: a story of travel and music.

    1. Fanshawe, David, 1942    2. Composers
Correspondence, reminiscences, etc.    I. Title.
ML410.F219A3        780'.92'4        75-2038
ISBN 0-8129-0560-1

Set in Monotype Bembo
Made and Printed in Great Britain

End Paper Maps by Tom Stalker-Miller

# Contents

# Illustrations

# *Foreword*

'Total cost £48 – Travel Expense £2.2.0 – Distance covered 12,000 miles.' Thus ended David Fanshawe's blow-by-blow account of his first 'mammoth adventure' to the Middle East in 1967. In 1969, before he set off on his journey which produced his *African Sanctus*, he wrote 'My vision is *Vast* and *Simple*. My music will *Communicate* a message of love, peace and faith in the *One God*' . . . 'I shall slip in by way of Cairo and fulfil a dream I have had since I was a small boy; who used to imagine that he was going to Africa as soon as his trunk was packed for school.'

David is perhaps the most original, independent and self-reliant young man I have known. An Eccentric; yet a good man, positive and full of purpose. A Visionary with the character and tenacity to convert his visions into reality. A Pioneer, Composer, Cameraman, Traveller, Recorder, Writer and Performer.

There is no knowing what great things this man may achieve in the next thirty years, and I would give much to live to see it.

Keith Falkner

12.iv.74.

# Author's Note

Sometimes I stand with my Cap on my head,
with endless song and glorious noises
shivering down my spine.
My life is full of Praise and my language is Music.

This book, which I like to call an Epistle, is a 'Secret'. It's the first Epistle according to the Apostle Fanshawe, a magical story about travel and music.

It's a Potato!

'The Potato' relates to an incident in my early childhood out of which grew a whole world of understanding – my family have known about it for years. I won't explain it all now, as that would only spoil the Autobiographical chapter to come.

Now, my family, known as 'Them at Home', consist of my mother who is called 'The Mouse', my father who is called 'The Father' or 'Our Father who art in Aldington' after his father, Grandfather Fan, who was known for many years as 'Our Father who art in Farnham'. And then of course there's Grandpa who is ninety-six, James 'The Brother' ten years my junior (Sub Lt. J. R. Fanshawe, R.N.), Tessa the dog, and George and Evelyn who do things for Them at Home.

Yes, I suppose I am a bit eccentric, but then so are most explorers. The only difference is that most of the others didn't try to compose their explorings into music. *African Sanctus* is a composition which puts the Mass into a new perspective. It's like an African song – for the world is full of song and I want to tell you about it.

Now my song is beginning to be sung because the Witch Doctors have persuaded me to sing it. As they rattled their stones and Secrets, part of the cures they use in the prescription of medicines for their patients, they told me to go away and learn something in a hurry – saying:

> Go and learn something
> Oh my Friend,
> Mr David –
> Go and learn something.
> HURRY!

*African Sanctus* is only part of the 'something in a hurry' – it's only part of the 'Ultimate Cure' which the Witch Doctors have the power to prescribe if they feel I deserve it.

> For I intend to fill my Egg Life with sail,
> enough to blow me round the Orient and back
>   to Praise Him
> who blew the wind straight to carry me there. . .

part of another Secret I wrote on one of my journeys to Them at Home, who now live in a converted smuggler's cottage in Kent.

At one time Them at Home used to live at Cedar Cottage in Camberley, as The Father was in the Army. I was brought up in a very military atmosphere. I don't live with 'Them' any more because I'm happily married to Judith who is, at the time of Epistolizing, expecting a baby. We live in East Sheen near darkest Mortlake where we belong when we're here – which would be as little as possible if I could help it!

So having put you in the picture, don't agitate if you keep reading about a Witch Doctor known as the Hippo Man, The Mouse, The Father etc. – they are just a normal part of the procedure.

> Ever since I have been Him,
> standing on a 'Chic Weed' gazing out to sea,
> I have longed to be in a place far away.
> It was always Africa.
> My trunk never went to school – it went to Africa.

The trouble was it took me twenty-seven years to get to Africa, with the financial help of the Ralph Vaughan Williams Trust (R.V.W. Trust). Their good initiative was followed by the Winston Churchill Memorial Trust who sent me where? To AFRICA – to do Adventure and Exploration!

*African Sanctus* – book, record, television film, and the ideas that it embraces – is the result. It's also the third work in a Trilogy of compositions which fuses the music in my head with the music I have recorded on my travels.

The whole story is a little magical because there are things in it which plunge me deep into a world of 'Other Things' which I understand, which the Witch Doctors certainly understand, if they are paying attention, and which the reader may well understand at the end of this Epistle.

Perhaps the most important Secret of all is the one said, with front teeth clenched, to The Mouse, who is known in the Secret as 'PUMP'. It is said with all the longing for Africa and the stampede in the Elephant Grass.

'PUMP, what lies beyond the hills?'

To which she has to reply: 'FIRST THE LAND and THEN THE SEA.'

This is the Secret which grew out of being a boy into being 'a being' – it's just that now I can come out with my Secrets because the Witch Doctors have said that I can. If I do not, the Secrets will be forgotten like the Songs of the Generations that have come and gone from the lands.

I'm telling you this so that in the pages following you too will clench your front teeth just like the Witch Doctors do who know the 'Ultimate Cure'.

Perhaps the Ultimate Cure is effort, doing one's best and asking oneself the question over and over again:

'What lies beyond the hills?'

Perhaps the Ultimate Cure is TRUTH in the imaginary Trial on the Hill of Eternity, opposite the Mountain of the Leopard. Some might even call it a Trial of Conscience before a formidable Court in the presence of the Eyes of Eternity: Witch Doctors, Elders and You, Members of the Jury and Greater Public, whose responsibility it is to decide if the evidence put before you is enough to set me free forever and forever. In other words – DO I COMMUNICATE?

It is a serious matter.

So here is my Evidence in the form of an autobiography and commentary on letters written on many lonely journeys, which I have now composed into an Epistle – not unlike a Symphony.

The whole thing is one big song which began a long time ago when I was born. That is why I am a Subject – for we are all Subjects. This makes the Witch Doctors very happy because it's wild, gay, abandoned, ritualistic, in the spirit of an African *ngoma* (a tribal get-together) in which there is a Patient who *must* be cured – HARAMBEE!*

The Trial is of course a chaotic one. The Hippo Man is Chief of the Court and the first piece of evidence, in case you are wondering what the drawing is, happens to be my signature. It represents me on a camel riding across the desert dreaming up music. In the head of the camel there is a treble clef and in the bottom of the camel there is a bass clef. I am to be seen on top of the camel, balanced a little precariously because I can't draw and because music is coming out of my head. On

---

*The spirit of Harambee, of working together, of helping one another.

top of my head is the Spirit Cap which has been blessed by the Witch Doctors. It's the Cap I have worn now for many years and was originally bought in Folkestone for 7s. 6d. I compose all my music wearing it, I travel in it, and cannot find a substitute for it. Some of you may have even seen it.

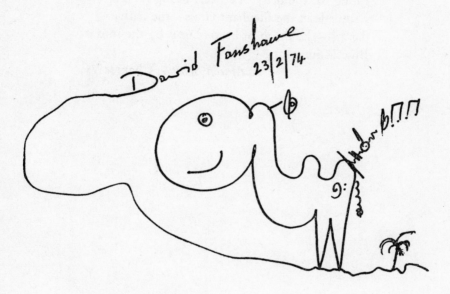

I long for the belly of Africa, I long for the stampede in the Elephant Grass – the native dances – the throb of hearts burnt by the sons of Blue Mountains.

*African Sanctus*, Chapter VII

# I

# Trial in the Eyes of Eternity

On the front of *African Sanctus* you can see the remarkable face of a man who represents in my eyes the symbolic figurehead of all the legends and myths of Africa – the Hippo Man. In real life he is a Luo Elder I discovered with the help of Chief Paul in a bar near Ahero on the road to Kisumu in Kenya.

As Chief of the Court the Hippo Man is surrounded by a fantastic array of colourful characters – some wearing magnificent ostrich plumes, others wearing dark blue pin-striped suits, military uniforms, nothing at all, wigs and cassocks, some with beards, others with no beards, but all with something of importance to say for themselves.

For days the people of the Court have been arriving on foot across the bush to the scene of the Trial which has been carefully selected by the Elders and Witch Doctors on the Hill of Eternity, which is to be found opposite the Mountain of the Leopard. The proceedings have been in progress for some time and the point has been reached where the Court has been subjected to several very uncomplimentary criticisms of my music, however the Court says that it would rather listen to a good story than puffs of wind which wouldn't even stir a lion out of its den.

The whole character of the Trial is based on personal experiences whilst sharing the lives of certain African peoples. My music, that is the music of the Defendant, is therefore of little importance. What matters is that there is something to discuss, and something to be important about. A critic on the *Financial Times* is just about to finish – all the things the critics say are quoted from actual reviews of the Defendant's music.

'But I also love African music: and Fanshawe's additions to and commentary on it seem to me in this case to be little more than vulgar excrescence.'

There followed a deathly silence in Court as the Witch Doctors, Elders, Members of the Jury and Greater Public gathered themselves together having been incensed by the words 'vulgar excrescence'. Then the Hippo Man continued to question the Jury as he drew in long and satisfying puffs upon his pot-pipe.

'Has Nairobi City Library been informed NOT to advertise the Defendant's vulgar excrescence?' he asked.

'It has M'Lud' replied the Jury.

'Good. Has *The Times* got anything useful to suggest either for or against the Defendant?'

'It has Your Honour – it's got a lot to suggest!' said Counsel for the Prosecution.

'Then I call upon Counsel to produce *The Times*' witness and hurry because *Time* is being wasted and *Time* doesn't like being wasted.'

*The Times*' witness obediently rose and took his learned seat in the witness box saying that he was a music critic for *The Times* sworn to tell the truth. He began – 'David Fanshawe must be an unusual case in that he is a composer whose music arises out of his foreign explorations. He has made several adventurous journeys in the Middle East and Africa, and his . . .'

No sooner had *The Times* begun, than half the Witch Doctors got up, yawned, scratched their heads and decided that it was time to go for a 'short call' (a polite way of saying in Africa that one must go and have a pee). But *The Times* carried on regardless as several Witch Doctors stood aside and squatted in the long grasses which surrounded the scene of the Trial. One or two of them turned the 'short call' into a 'long call', and one or two others discussed the business of a cow which had been stolen from some unfortunate European's farm in which a farm labourer had been speared to death by Warrior Raiders. Bravely *The Times* went on to say:

'Sometimes the result is merely incongruous, as in the *Pater Noster*, where too quickly are we switched from a lament recorded by Lake

Kyoga to the ambience of an English cathedral. Or in the final . . .'

'Thank you Mr Times . . .' interrupted the Hippo Man who turned to the tobacco-chewing Witch Doctors and solemnly asked them what they thought a 'Pater Noster' actually was?

'It's the Lord's Prayer,' said Counsel for the Defence, 'and the Defendant has subsequently dropped the movement and recomposed it in English because he says that down near Lake Victoria they all speak English in the mission schools. He suggests the Court listens to the Lord's Prayer in its rightful place within the context of *African Sanctus*.'

Upon the word 'Sanctus' the entire courtroom was again filled with the magic of rattling stones and Secrets which the Witch Doctors shook as they muttered:

> Sanctus, Sanctus, Sanctus,
> Dominus Deus Sabaoth.
> Go and learn something,
> Oh my Friend,
> Mr David –
> Go and learn something.
> HURRY!

Now the Defendant was quite obviously upset – very upset – and it seemed at the time that there was no hope so he hastened back to Africa to 'Go and learn something in a hurry' as the Witch Doctors had advised.

'Court adjourned – adjourned until the Defendant has finished his walking in Africa,' said the Hippo Man.

The Court was adjourned for a very long time indeed and during it many things were discussed at length as the Witch Doctors had a great deal of curing to do because of the oncoming rains and because of all the Circumcisions and Marriages which had to be arranged. When the Defendant returned, however, after his walking in Africa – nearly a year later – he went on to walk in America to talk about it all before returning to the Court.

'Order! The Defendant is returning and says he has learnt something!' announced the Hippo Man with a fuss.

'The Defendant will rise and will remain risen until further notice,' said the Municipal Armory (the Hill of Eternity's Heraldry).

The Defendant rose and adjusted the Spirit Cap on his head which by this time had been praised and blessed in an Initiation Ceremony of the Pokot, a remote tribe in the Cherangany Hills of Kenya. Both the Cap and the Defendant looked much the worse for wear after such a long walk round Africa and America.

'This is indeed cause for celebrations and fresh tobacco,' said the Hippo Man triumphantly as the Defendant (the Patient in the eyes of the Witch Doctors) produced several pounds' worth of fresh tobacco which he had brought all the way from Virginia. The Municipal Armory handed it out with a few monetary notes which didn't seem to be quite enough monetary notes to satisfy everybody in the court-room.

'We call upon Mr Earl Arnett of *The Sun*, Baltimore, America, to give evidence M'Lud,' said Counsel for the Defence as a complete hush descended over the Court and the crinkling of monetary notes ceased. Mr Arnett, speaking with a warm American accent, entered the witness box.

'Contrary to the old colonial prejudices,' said Earl Arnett, 'the musical consciousness of the African is surely equal to the European. Only the techniques are different, but as Mr Fanshawe remarkably demonstrates, they can be welded harmonically into something very contemporary and important . . . It was extraordinarily beautiful . . .'

'Just a minute, Mr Baltimore,' interrupted the Hippo Man as the Witch Doctors turned to each other and spoke in hushed whispers, leaning on their sticks. 'We would all like to know what the Swahili word is for "beautiful"?'

'Musiki ya ki Afrika mitamu-mzuri!' replied the Defendant, which definitely satisfied the curiosity of the Witch Doctors who were having difficulties understanding an American accent.

'Which kingdom are you the Earl of?' asked the Hippo Man who continued to puff away on his pot-pipe, but Earl Arnett ignored the question and continued to give evidence patiently.

'The music demonstrates to all what a few have always known – that so-called primitive and civilized people . . .'

'OBJECTION Your Honour! The word PRIMITIVE is an insult to society!' said Counsel for the Prosecution.

'Objection sustained. Thank you – er – Earl of Baltimore. Any more witnesses?' asked the Hippo Man.

At which point there seemed to be a demonstration going on in Court for an angry young man suddenly leapt into the air, shouting abuse at the Defendant, saying that he once heard him talking on the BBC. The saboteur then produced a pistol and pressing it hard into the Defendant's neck screwed him up by the arm and dragged him forward to the feet of the Hippo Man. All the Elders and Witch Doctors huddled together, rattled their sticks and blew their noses with their fingers, spitting on the courtroom floor at the same time.

'What is this? What is this you are doing?' asked the Hippo Man. 'I will not have court-jacking going on in this courtroom. Who are you? Are you going to shoot the Defendant? If so do it quickly and we'll send him off to the Mountain of the Leopard – otherwise drop your weapon, sit down and give evidence in the way to which we are accustomed. Were you trained at Sandhurst?'

The court-jacker glared at Counsel for the Defence, stuffed the pistol into his back trouser pocket and began to give a lengthy explanation of why he hated the Defendant and his music so much, during which time the Hippo Man fell asleep.

'I was offended by your quite shameless self-advertisement . . .'

'OBJECTION! An artist has to live, M'Lud,' replied Counsel for the Defence.

Counsel was not answered as the Hippo Man had fallen into a deep sleep. 'Your Honour! We've just received a telex from Australia!' Again there was a scuffle at the back of the courtroom as a telex was handed from one Witch Doctor to another but by the time it got to the Hippo Man, who had been rudely woken up, it was covered in tobacco stains and hardly readable – which didn't really make any difference. It was looked at, considered, but of course, it wasn't read out! Meanwhile the court-jacker got down, having been persuaded to do so by the other Witch Doctors who automatically spared him a piece of their tobacco for having entertained them and for having said all that he had said.

The next witness caused an even greater sensation.

'Our next witness not only took the trouble to introduce the Defendant to Bwana Collins and Memsaab Villiers (the publishers of this Epistle), but he has taken the trouble to come all the way from Nairobi City to the Hill of Eternity to give evidence. We call upon Bwana John Eames, Editor-in-Chief of our famous magazine *Africana*,' said Counsel for the Defence.

No sooner had Bwana John entered the witness box than many of the Witch Doctors, recognizing him, stood up, leaning on their sticks, and expressed their astonishment at finding Bwana John in such an unlikely place. They even shook their long, pierced ear lobes with delight as Bwana John began to speak to them.

'My own introduction to David Fanshawe indicates the type of man he is. He had been walking in a Nairobi suburban street, saw a grand piano through a window, walked in and introduced himself to the house servant as a friend of the Bwana's . . .'

'Bwana!' exclaimed the Hippo Man, who was now fully awake, 'Can you confine your comments to the question at hand, namely the Defendant's music, and tell us why he has done what he has done?'

Bwana John said he would rather leave the serious musical appreciation of the Defendant's music to a serious music critic, but he did add that fame or at least appreciation of the Defendant's talents, was catching up with him in Africa.

'Fame?' questioned the Hippo Man. 'The Eyes of Eternity are not interested in fame. What is more important to everyone present is whether or not the Defendant's music brings on the rainy season and a fruitful harvest, so that our people and our cattle have enough to eat – next witness!'

'Possibly the most bizarre composition of the year...' said the *Guardian*.

'Mr Guard,' snapped the Hippo Man as the Witch Doctors, on hearing the word 'bizarre' began to take out their curses and swears, threatening that they would put a curse on *all* critics unless everything was going to be all right and that all poverty would be expelled so that they might sing. 'I feel I should remind you that in these times of drought in which we find ourselves living, many of our cattle are dying. Many of our young children go without milk. Many of our Warriors have been denied the pleasure of raiding by the Government. We are prepared to listen to what you have to say but we need no persuasion to go to the "Bazaar" as we have few monetary notes these days with which to purchase the things we really need. Can you tell us about the Defendant's music, because if the Eyes of Eternity find him NOT guilty then we might all share in the rewards.' At which point a very learned professor of music whose name was Wilfrid Mellers, ambled up and spoke a great piece of oratory. Now the oratory itself was so long and erudite about the Defendant's music, that during its length there wasn't a murmur. Instead, the Witch Doctors, recognizing the skills and talents which they themselves possessed, stopped chewing and listened spell-bound to the Great White Doctor from York University. They put away their curses and swears and tucking their long, dark overcoats under their bony knees crouched with satisfaction and waited patiently for the oration to finish as they leant upon their sticks. Not one single Elder went off into the long grasses and the Hippo Man, whose eyes remained wide open throughout, stared at the Doctor of Learning as he chewed upon his pot-pipe.

This is how The Professor ended his speech:

'...Though Fanshawe makes the African musical experience relevant to our world, he leaves us feeling pitifully vulnerable. It seems that if we Europeans are to relinquish the qualities that a Beethoven most heroically represents, we must be prepared to cut sorry figures in competition with the Africans.'

Now after Wilfrid Mellers had finished, instead of applauding in the usual manner associated with the Western World, each and every Witch Doctor began a great and wonderful song in which they praised first of all themselves, then the Patient Mr David, the Great White Doctor from York University, and the Hippo Man, who they said had once speared a Hippopotamus in a place very far away and killed it with a single thrust. They then went on to praise, in their usual manner, each and every critic with a special mention for the 'angry one who fired a gun' and the one who said that 'beer was flowing in the bazaar, beer was flowing . . .'

It was a magnificent song but sadly the Patient, who longed to record it, had left his tape-recorder in darkest Mortlake not expecting there to be any music at the Trial – which only goes to show that one should always be ready and waiting, for every day is worth recording.

Every day is a day of Praise and of History.

Finally with great dignity the Hippo Man rose from his seat at the Head of the Court and asked the women to bring on plentiful supplies of beer and extra pounds of tobacco. He then spoke to the Defendant saying:

'Mr David, can you tell us how you came here, where you have come from and what it is you want?'

# II

# *Fanshawe's Autobiographical*

*Con Humoresque*

I was born in an air-raid in Paignton, Devon, during the Second World War and the bomb which might have hit me and The Mouse hit the railway station instead – almost killing The Father (he says), who nobly threw himself upon a lucky 'Wren' as the bomb went off on the other side of the station platform. That was in 1942 while The Father was visiting his new-born son for the first time.

I was a Potato – a whimsical being of magic loneliness.*

Earliest recollections are of ME sitting in the bath singing 'Over the Rainbow'. The Mouse says I sang in tune at nine months – but it didn't do me much good!

I was a Potato.

My musical career started at the keyboard when I was six, and the first piece I ever learnt was called 'Waddling Ducks'. My first music teacher was called Miss Young.

When *not* playing 'Waddling Ducks', I imagined myself going to Africa, and whenever anybody came to tea – that usually meant The Grannies, for my two grandmothers were sisters, making The Father and The Mouse first cousins – I used to have elaborate exhibitions in my bedroom and have always been known as a bit of an exhibitionist ever since. For years I never understood the difference between an *exhibition* and an *expedition*, not unlike Winnie-the-Pooh.

Potato.

In 1947 The Father, Lt.Col. R. A. R. Fanshawe, then serving as a regular soldier, built us a wooden 'Colt' cottage in Camberley, Surrey, which ought to have a plaque on it saying that we lived there. It looked

* See the Potato Story

exactly like a loaf of brown bread and still stands today. Contrary to all pessimists Cedar Cottage did not burn down and can be found in Watchett's Drive on the left as you go up from the Frimley Road in the avenue of fir trees. It was there, when not away at school, that I grew up in a world of my own, completely oblivious of others, obsessed with exhibitions, tea parties and secret places I used to touch on a radiator in the nursery. I was ashamed of this for many years and never told anyone about the 'Touching of the Radiator' until I discovered a famous Witch Doctor who always used to touch a certain root every time he prescribed medical cures.

'I touch this place in the name of Orient-Are, when will I return?' This magical Secret I would repeat over and over again as the radiator was touched with the left index finger, especially on the last few agonizing days of the holidays. How I came upon 'in the name of Orient-Are' is a bit of a mystery but it might have had something to do with 'We three Kings of Orient are' and Sandhurst Chapel. During the holidays we used to go to Sandhurst Chapel every Sunday.

Potato, 'in the name of Orient-Are'.

*St George's Choir School, Windsor Castle, Berks.*
Aged eight Master David failed to get into St George's choir (The Choir), unlike his musical brother ten years later, who became head chorister – what a wasted career. The Brother (Sub Lt. J. R. Fanshawe, R.N.) now roams the high seas with a permanent hacking cough it seems.

'Doc H', the famous organist and choirmaster Sir William Harris, said after choir trial: 'Fanshawe sings perfectly in tune, but he lacks volume and is a bit slow on the uptake.'

Mr Cleave, the Headmaster, nicknamed me 'Taxi' or 'Taxicab' because my ears stuck out and he said I reminded him of a taxi with its doors left open.

Having failed to become a chorister, I automatically became what is known as 'a Super', for all non-choristers at St George's wore blue ties whereas The Choir were distinguished by their red ties and clever looks.

I was broken into prep school life by Wylam, who was assigned the task of looking after me, as he had already been at St George's for a term and knew the ropes. The first sentence I wrote home on Sunday was

'Dear Mummy and Daddy.
I hope you are well.
Ever since you left me there standing like a Weeping Willow . . .'*

I never really knew what happened to Wylam, except that I believe in real life he did become a tree doctor. He also spent some time in Aldershot Cemetery working as a grave digger. Wylam do get in touch.

How I used to fear Monday mornings. Gym, wrestling, cold, icy, purple knees in the gym – and more and more wrestling.

Mrs Cleave saw rather a lot of me my first winter term as I suffered from terrible chilblains which gnawed to my very bones, you know! In the evenings after 'lights out', Mrs Cleave would rub my hands with a thick, black cream. This I enjoyed partly because the cream really did soothe the rawness of the fingers and partly because I enjoyed Mrs Cleave's company and the excuse to go and sit with her on the sofa in their beautiful drawing room which all St George's boys will remember with affection. Also it meant I escaped dormitory pranks – 'U.B.C.' (the 'Under Bed Club'), which involved horrid little boys trying to break the record, sliding on their rugs round and round the dormitory under the beds – SNEAK!

Such pranks I really didn't care for. Thank you, Mrs Cleave.

---

* The 'Weeping Willow' letter would have to be the one that got lost, but reproduced is another typical Potato Letter written at the same time in 1951 when I was nine. You will notice, of course, the spelling and its translation !

## *Potato Letter from St George's – 1951*

Dear Mummy and Daddy.
I hope you are well.
I am sorry to say that you're not
allowed to have comics.
The church,* is simply lovely.
It has got lovely statues all round it.
It is miles better than Sandhurst.
Sunday
LOVE

Please send me some more
stamps.

Please can you send me some
more writing paper.

\* St George's Chapel.

## St George's Chapel

Going up the 'Hundred Steps', a lovely climb to Windsor Castle, through the Chapter Gardens and into the Castle residence to St George's Chapel I shall never forget. The chapel made a tremendous impact on me and even in *African Sanctus* influences can be traced back to those memorable Sundays when we, as small prep school boys, would stand in our allotted pews overlooking The Choir, Military Knights, and other castle residents. I remember how I used to gaze up at the beautiful ceiling of the chapel and listen to The Choir singing. In many ways I am thankful I failed to get into the choir as I could have developed a lot faster than I did, which might have altered the entire course of my life. Instead I held The Choir in great awe and remained a contented Super.

Potato.

Later on in the Chapter Greenhouse I had a passion for breeding Moon Moths. I bred them in glass cages and was known throughout the school as 'Fanshawe and his Moon Moths!'

Minter F. said he knew how to kill and mount Moon Moths properly. A killing jar, which 'Mato', the Matron, won't forget, was brought to the school by The Father from Harrods. On the appropriate day, when the unfortunate Moon Moth had hatched out, the killing jar was duly fetched from Mato's cupboard, where she kept the malt, and Minter F. down in the potting shed proceeded to do the killing and the mounting with an excited audience of little boys who jumped up and down shouting, 'Fanshawe and his Moon Moths!' Result? The whole school got a piece of Moon Moth and Minter F.'s attempts failed.

Many times I used to sit on the Banks of the Chapter, under the stone walls of Windsor Castle, and imagine huge Moon Moths flapping about in India. I had been brought up on stories of India as my Father, Grandfather and Great-Grandfather, who was once the Postmaster General of India, had all been born in the vicinity of Poona.

'Moon Moths come from the hills, darling,' Granny Fan used to say. Unfortunately my Moon Moths came from L. Hugh Newman of Kent.

Moon Moths, like exhibitions, tea parties and later, The Puppets, were yet another obsession. Hardly an hour went by without the words 'Moon Moths' being mentioned.

The last of the Moon Moths hatched out in the Chapter Greenhouse in the spring of 1953 and this time was carefully preserved by Dr Willcox, father of Willcox, a fellow Super, who pinned it out and presented it to me in a glass cabinet. Owing to the generosity of Mr Cleave in collaboration with Dr Willcox and the dead Moon Moth, the whole school was awarded a half-holiday on account of 'Fanshawe and his Moon Moths'.

Then came the summer and our annual holiday to East Wittering, the autumn, the Christmas holidays and then the Potato Story.

## The Potato Story

*A little symphonic poem – poco mesto e dolce e tragico*
I was aged about ten in the middle of winter on a cold, dark evening during the Christmas holidays at Cedar Cottage. There was deep snow on the ground and Cedar Cottage looked more like a Christmas cake in the middle of Canada than a loaf of brown bread. The Father was away, or was out, or hadn't returned from London, I cannot remember. The Mouse sat by a blazing fire in the drawing room. When I walked into the room, early that evening, I spied on top of the gramophone one solitary, shrivelled potato with a little root sticking out of it. How it got there no one will ever know. Suddenly, feeling desperately sad for the potato, I picked it up and went and sat beside The Mouse gazing at the potato in my hand. The fire roared in the grate.

'Why don't you put it on the fire?' said The Mouse.

So, carefully, I placed the potato in the middle of the fire with the aid of a poker. For a few stunned moments we both sat in absolute silence. Afraid to move, in case I might show the tears which were beginning to blur my eyes, I remained quite motionless and imagined the burning agony of the potato suffering in the fire. Then, I remembered the snow outside. So, seized with emotion, as only a small boy can be, I rushed at the potato with the poker and extricated it from the fire, bursting into floods of tears all at the same time. Hastily throwing open the French windows, I flung the burning potato as far as I could into the deep snow of the garden to try and cool it down. The potato sank about four inches into the snow and as I watched by the light from the drawing room window, I saw a little hole in the snow where the potato had fallen.

I cried and I cried and I cried.

It was so sad and I wished there had never been a potato on top of the gramophone. Of course it never occurred to me what the potato might have suffered had I eaten it!

And that is the potato story. For many years it was one of the Secrets between me and The Mouse, who you will also remember is known as PUMP in the other Secret. Perhaps I should explain a little bit more about what I think 'a Potato' actually is, because the 'Potato feeling' is very important to me.

When you have seen a Potato, you have in fact seen something very touching, generally in the form of a person. 'The Person' is usually alone, dejected, or sad looking – but Potato Sadness is sadness which touches the heart almost to breaking point. Here is another example which only happened the other day. You might object, but I can't help feeling a Potato when I see one and I would like to share the feeling with you, since it's not often that you would be asked to share the 'Potato feeling' with anyone else but me.

Not so long ago, upon the cliffs of Folkestone, one of my favourite haunts apart from Africa, I saw two 'Potatoes'. They were very happy, obviously enjoying themselves, perfectly unaware that I was watching but I was. Both the Potatoes were slightly handicapped in speech and movement and were happily playing football with Mum and Dad looking on from the car. Very shortly, Mum came down and said:

'Would you like your orange now boys?'

Whereupon the Potatoes abandoned the football and went to sit on a bench on the cliff top. Suddenly the Potato feeling came over me very strongly indeed and I was reminded of a day I had spent in the Lotikipi Plains having collapsed from exhaustion on a sixty mile walk in

Turkana country in Northern Kenya. In the end I was rescued by Father Leo after my guide had gone back to Kakuma to get help.

The Potatoes, however, upon the cliffs of Folkestone, so very far away from the Lotikipi plains, continued to sip their orange squash from plastic cups. I noticed how happy and carefree they were.

'Would you like to play football again?' asked Mum, 'then finish up your orange.'

Now it was the size of the cups of orange squash which affected me more than anything else; for an exhausted traveller in the African bush the cups were only enough for one gulp taken without breath and yet, there were the Potatoes on the cliffs of Folkestone continuing to sip so slowly, unaware of real thirst or the unfortunate person looking on. The person left having gazed across the sea to the hills of France and the lands beyond, saying to himself – 'Potato'.

## The Puppets

*A tempo Passepied – (A lively French dance of the 17th Century)*
There was a time when our whole lives revolved around 'The Puppets'.

Puppet shows took the place of exhibitions. Now the Grannies would come to tea and see the latest puppet show. These, 'Fanshawe and his Puppets', I used to write, direct and produce with a small company, and it is here that I would like to introduce Willy Bordass and The Vics.

Willy Bordass was quite brilliant when it came to electric trains and lighting puppet theatres. Willy's parents lived in Malaya and 'poor old Willy' sometimes used to come and spend the holidays with us. Since then I haven't seen Willy who now, I believe, is a scientist. Have you seen Willy Bordass, Members of the Jury? In those days Willy's trains used to ramble all over Cedar Cottage and transformers with hundreds of bulbs would be permanently On Test before they were installed in the puppet theatre – usually the night before a show. Willy and I used to visit Woolworth's nearly every day for more wire or for more powerful bulbs.

A puppet show would take about a year to produce and was usually performed in April around my birthday on 19 April, Primrose Day, when all the daffodils were out. The Puppet Theatre was built in the carpentry shop at St George's and was decorated with gold braid which was stuck on the top of it by a very kind man who owned a wood shop in Park Street.

The Vics were press-ganged into 'The Puppets' every year – until the time that Jennifer Hilary (the well-known actress) swept us all off our feet, aged about fifteen.

Productions included – *Jack and the Beanstalk, Ali Baba and the Forty Thieves* (I could never spell it right), *Babes in the Wood, Mother Goose* – all shows which we put on in the Nursery at Cedar Cottage. The Brother has written *his* memoirs upon The Puppets:

'Being ten years younger than the real author of this "episthole" (as these sort of things are always known as in our family), I was only about five in the heyday of "The Puppets". For many months the happy clan of puppeteers would gather at Cedar Cottage for rehearsals, script readings, prop-buildings and all the other arrangements that *had* to be done to mount the show. I was never involved, or to be more precise, I was never allowed to be involved. This had disastrous consequences, of which the most important was that I could not get into my bedroom/playroom/nursery, as it had become "The Theatre". This made me furious and The Mouse must have spent many hours trying to shut up a bawling mini-Fanshawe! Sometimes I got my own back and would sneak in to have a look round, invariably moving something out of place. Whether I had or not, I was always given the blame.

Sometimes my patience would be rewarded. This would normally happen close to the performances when the pitch of excitement was getting too intense for even my elder brother to bear. He would sneak up to our "bodroom" ("e" in our family is pronounced as "o") and demonstrate the stage lighting or his latest puppet. This for me really made the waiting worthwhile as I then at last felt a part of the team. Of course the inevitable would happen on the actual day. All the Grannies would arrive and by the time they had found their seats there would be only one person still without. But never mind, I always managed to see one half of the stage and always felt superior to the rest of the family because I had seen it in the making. Brothers were taught at an early age to suffer in silence!'

Here ends The Brother.

## Coffee in the High Street

*Agitato – to meet for coffee in the High Street*
There was me, Simon Pope, Brian O'Flaherty and Philip (the Jealous) with Angela Pringle and Jennifer Hilary. We were loathed. Simon had a motorbike which I rode pillion and Philip the Jealous, because of his age, rode up the High Street on a bicycle.

Angela and Jennifer were sensational and everybody knew it – including all the Dads. There was something about Angela and Jennifer, they were idolized. In fact, in the end, we lost them to Sandhurst. Both were to become famous; Angela as a fashion model and Jennifer, as I have already mentioned, a very successful actress. Simon and Brian went into the Army, Philip the Jealous became a playboy, I think, and Fanshawe of course – a Composer and Explorer. Those were the days of parties and more parties and very little music except jazz.

At Aldershot Club dances, I used to play the piano when the band went out and all the girls used to come round and swoon! But in my private self I suffered a lot, as I had a terrible inability to improvise at the keyboard. I didn't seem to have a natural aural and harmonic sense like other pianists, and this really hampered me – especially at Christmas parties when I was the one they always picked on to play 'God Save the Queen', and Christmas Carols in E major.

I couldn't sight-read then, still can't sight-read and even worse I was musically illiterate. Despite my expensive education I never had a single lesson in harmony and theory and any visions I had of exploring Africa were drowned in the happy, carefree, breezy days of Club dances and self-conceit.

I was at the time a Stoic.

## Chandos House, Stowe, Bucks.

My first journey to Egypt took place when I went 'to Egypt' after a somewhat painful three-day search to find it, having discovered that 'Egypt' at Stowe School meant the lavatories! They were in fact named after the so-called Egyptian Entrance and had once been used as stables in the time of the Duke of Buckingham – I think.

I remember it well. In Form 4C a boy stuck up his hand and said to our form master, Mr Fox:

'Please sir, can I go to Egypt?'

At the time I was bottom of 4C and 4C was of course the bottom form in the school.

Oh well I thought, what a lucky boy on the first day of term to be going to Egypt. I wonder why he's bothered to come back to school at all?

Stowe days were rosy days. I got out of playing rugger by playing squash, and in the summer there was, of course, tennis with my friend Behar down by the Palladian Bridge. There was also 'Corps'.

My fear at Stowe was 'Pits'. This meant you went *up-sighling* (forgotten how to spell *sighling*) or was it *down-sighling*? Anyway it involved a horrible sandpit with a fence at the top to which one was attached by a rope, somewhere near the 'British Worthies'.*

'Fanshawe, don't look down – keep your head up you 'orrible little man!'

Having got to the bottom of the sandpit, one was then expected to RUN all the way up the side of it again (madness!) into the Bourbon Fields, past the Bourbon Tower to do 'Walls'. All part of one's military training in the C.C.F. (Combined Cadet Force). The only thing I did enjoy about the C.C.F. was polishing my boots and marching up and down the South Front because it reminded me of General Gordon marching up and down the Nile.

Apart from all that, my career at Stowe passed away in a daze of happiness and wishful thinking.

* Famous statues to be found in the grounds of Stowe near 'the Pits'.

On the musical front I did nothing very much – I played the piano, slightly better than other aspiring school pianists, but far preferred to practise jazz in the Musical Director's Study, especially on the week-ends. My particular favourite was Fats Waller's 'Alligator Crawl'. This was frowned upon.

'You are a conceited little boy,' snarled my terrifying Head of House, after an impromptu performance of 'Alligator Crawl' on the forbidden grand piano in the Assembly Hall just before lunch one day.

'You will take a school defaulter' (extra PT).

Redeeming my somewhat unorthodox career, and due to nothing short of brilliant cramming from the Geography Tutor, Mr Hunt, now the famous Headmaster of Roedean, I managed to pass seven 'O' Levels and Geography 'A' Level in the winter term because Stowe is in Buckinghamshire and during the summer term it must have had the highest pollen count in the entire realm of the diminishing British Empire. If anyone else suffers from hay fever as badly as I do, especially when taking their 'O' and 'A' Levels, I strongly advise a dose of Africa.

All I wanted to do at the time was to join the film industry, become a film director and go filming in Africa. So I went for an interview to the BBC and was asked what I thought was an idiotic question.

'What experience have you had in the film industry?'

Surely the interviewer *must* have known I had come specially to see him from school?

'None,' I replied, 'but I have produced, written and directed several puppet plays.'

'Then I strongly advise you to go away, get experience and come back and see me in three years' time,' said the man from the BBC – typical!

Finally I managed to secure another interview with the director of a documentary film company in London, who couldn't have cared less if I had been educated or not. I was accepted and triumphantly returned to Stowe for my last happy days, little realizing that an extraordinary meeting one eventful afternoon on practically the last day of term *would* affect the entire course of my life.

The balance of fate hangs upon a thin thread.

## The Baroness

*Serioso*

Fanshawe, whose number at Stowe was 421, was 'discovered' so to speak, one Speech Day, a sunny afternoon in July 1959, showing off in the music room with the windows wide open.

Fats Waller's 'Alligator Crawl' boogy-woogied up the pathway at fever pitch in hot competition with the Organ Voluntary as parents came out of Chapel.

It was terrific and had I not been prone to 'showing off', I might never have become 'a musician after all' – as The Mouse likes to put it. Suddenly a total stranger from a milling mob of passers-by stuck her head through the open window of the music room and *demanded* to know what I was playing. Delighted, I ushered her in. She was quite obviously unmoved by Fats Waller.

'Do you play Bach? Do you study the exercises of Czerny?' she questioned. Czerny, I subsequently learnt, only too well, was once the teacher of Liszt and terror of all would-be student pianists.

'Unfortunately not,' I replied, 'but I have just won the school music prize with my Debussy. Would you like to hear it?'

So, leaning over the keyboard and adjusting her glasses the stranger condescended to listen as I began what I thought was a wonderful rendition of a piece every aspiring school pianist has in his repertoire, namely the Prelude called – 'La Cathédrale engloutie'.

As I banged and crashed and imagined the waters of the sea covering the submerged cathedral with distant bells clanging under the waters, I thought to myself: 'Gee, I'm making a hit here!'

The last ripples washed away, the performance came to an end and then in raptures, I at last sat back and awaited the tremendous ovation . . .

'Thank you, but it is quite clear to me that you do not even know HOW to put your hands on the keyboard!' said the stranger. Those were her very words. Of course there followed a ghastly silence.

37

'What are you going to do when you leave school?' she asked. 'What is your name?'

. . . And that was how it all began.

The stranger who popped her head into the music room after Chapel spent the rest of the afternoon with me and revealed that she was Baroness Guirne van Zuylen. 'David,' she said, 'you are so naive, you know nothing. We shall have to start at the beginning – it's your muscles that need strengthening.'

She implied the muscles in my hands, wrists, fingers and arms that needed strengthening in order to become a pianist. At that stage we were merely talking about the piano and how to play the piano. But as we walked around the beautiful grounds of Stowe the Baroness inspired me. She gave me a new insight into music and talked about the techniques from which I would slowly emerge as a professional 'musician after all'. The Baroness left me standing there, no longer a weeping willow. She left me on my last day at school with a burning ambition. To go and study the piano with her in London once a week as soon as I started my first job as a trainee editor in the film industry.

S O.

From an 'ignorant, self-opinionated creep' quoting Sandhurst Cadets who threw me into the bushes and pulled my trousers off at the Aldershot Club during the Tennants' dance in the summer holidays of 1959, I suddenly realized, just in time, that I was truly a nobody.

*Frustrato e con molto apologetico*

My first sight of the Mediterranean was with Joel Lerner and his father as their guest. Joel was the grandson of the late Lord Marks and another contemporary at Stowe, and the following incident must be mentioned.

Having spent my childhood longing to be an explorer, I was naturally thrilled with the idea of going to the South of France. My family weren't able to afford those kind of luxury holidays. I bought a Paxette Camera and mention the incident with considerable apology, but it has to do with 'the longings' and is another Potato Story if you like.

It was on a Sunday morning in Monte Carlo when the film in my camera jammed. It was a disaster and being Sunday all the camera shops were shut. With a 'bee-in-me-bonnet' I searched everywhere for a darkroom, having a terrible urge to photograph the magnificent mountains which rose above the town. For the first time in my life I really felt I was 'abroad'.

Now the yacht which Joel's father had chartered had come into Monte Carlo from St Tropez and Joel's grandparents were then staying at the Hôtel de Paris. Suddenly it struck me that, if anywhere, I might find a dark cupboard in his grandfather's bedroom. So, borrowing the key from the concierge I announced myself as Joel's friend. The concierge agreed to let me have the key and there, just as I had expected was a most acceptable cupboard – just what I wanted. Shoving all the dresses to one side and removing all the shoes, forgetting that such a cupboard could hardly have belonged to a grandfather, I erected a chair inside and shut myself in with the camera. Success – there wasn't a chink of light! The problem, thank God, was only a simple one – the perforations of the 35 mm film had been torn. Quickly I moved the film on, jumped out, doing my best to avoid crumpling all the dresses, arranged everything as I had found it, quickly took some 'stock shots' of the mountains from the bedroom window and left having drunk a glass of Evian water as it was rather hot.

Returning the key to the concierge I made my way down to the Hôtel de Paris beach, hitching a ride in the residents' bus, claiming that I was, of course, a resident.

But unfortunately, the following day, the crime caught up with me.

'David,' said Joel's father, down by the swimming pool, 'I would like to have a word with you' – and a cold shiver ran down my spine.

'Did you go into the private apartments of Lady Marks yesterday?'

'Yes,' I replied, trying to explain about the camera.

'David, you are supposed to be my guest. I am responsible for you. Is it your normal practice to break into people's bedrooms and leave them as if a burglar had been through them? Lady Marks got quite a shock when she found all her shoes piled up in a corner and her dresses all crumpled.'

'Her shoes, her shoes, damn!' I said to myself.

'Now what sort of an upbringing have you had? Were you not taught any manners at Stowe? Would you do that sort of thing in your own parents' home?'

I thought for a moment of the higgledy-piggledy muddle at Cedar Cottage which all seemed a very long way away.

'I'm afraid I am going to have to send you home early, because it seems you cannot behave and I cannot take responsibility for you here. Now I want you to go and apologize to Lady Marks straight away.'

This I did, and much to my amazement was invited to lunch at the same time. Lord and Lady Marks were sitting by the swimming pool eating rounds of cold beef.

'You know David,' said Lord Marks, 'when I was your age I had an ambition – I felt that in my lifetime I would like to see every girl in England have the opportunity of feeling like a queen.' Those were his sentiments if not his exact words. If ever there was a man who lived to see his ambitions come to fruition Lord Marks must be that man. He was undoubtedly the first great man I ever met and happily I am reminded of him every time I go and buy my underpants at Marks and Spencer's store. I only hope they open up in Nairobi City for the benefit of everyone here present at this Trial.

## The Suite of Digs

*Squalido e poco miserio down to earthio*

Now the way in which one should perform any 'Suite of Digs' as a penniless batchelor in London is to realize that one changes tempo very frequently and that each movement represents a different landlady.

London life started for me in Holland Park in the autumn of 1959 at a hostel in which I shared a room with four lads from the North of England. All were older than myself. Not surprisingly on the first evening, as I walked down Holland Road from Notting Hill Gate, I found that all my sheets and blankets had been chucked out into the road, my bed was upside down on the landing, a spare pair of pants 'from-you-know-where' were hanging on the flagpole and a suitcase of personal effects was floating in a bath of cold water. Reason? Because when I first met the four lads from the North I happened to say, 'How do you do', which obviously didn't do at all!

After nine months of working as a glorified teaboy and first class postal service for Green Park Productions at 53 New Oxford Street, above the old umbrella shop, I was posted, thankfully, to Merton Park Film Studios in South Wimbledon s.w.19.

My second landlady's husband had once been a professional horn player who had recently died. Her real name was Mrs Button, but I nicknamed her Countess Mountbutton because she cooked the best pork chops I ever had and because we liked each other.

My boss at Merton Park Studios was the supervising editor of the Film Producers' Guild, known throughout the industry as 'Sago'.

I had been made assistant to Mr Sagovsky and gained valuable experience 'handling celluloid' which was to prove, in future years, of vital importance.

When I left the film industry and finally became a composer, I found that my knowledge and understanding of how films were made contributed tremendously not only to the craft of writing film music, but in the technical approach to problems that were to arise 'in the field' when recording folk music. The quality of my African recordings has often been praised for their stereophonic clarity. I attribute this, and possibly my own conception of musical composition, to the knowledge I gained at an early age as a film editor.

A composition like *African Sanctus* is in fact a kind of musical documentary, because it teaches and informs both the listener and performer about African music and its relationship to Western music and composition. At the same time I hope it captures something of the eternal soul of music, which I find profoundly mystical and moving, and which it is taking me an awful long time to attain.

First of all I had to learn how to put the dots down on paper!

## How I Began to Write Music

*Lento (Slowly)*

During the time I worked in films, I continued to have one piano lesson a week with the Baroness in her mews house in St John's Wood, N.W.8, and was becoming quite a fanatical pianist, being encouraged to enter for various London Music Festivals. Aged eighteen, however, early in the New Year of 1960, I thought I had fallen in love with a girl called Jill. Unfortunately it didn't last very long as her mother soon requested that I shouldn't see her any more, unless we were in company with other friends, because I was a gentile. This hit me so hard at the time that I vowed I would express my unrequited passions in a work of art.

Walking back, a seemingly pathetic young gentile, towards Golders Green Tube Station, my heart torn, my head pounding, I thought to myself:

'What can I do? How can I express my love for Jill? I can't write, I can't paint; I can't see her any more, I play the piano, but can't write dots down on paper – what can I do? Oh Jill, Oh Jill, o h!'

But on arrival at South Wimbledon, standing on the station platform, as these things usually happen, it suddenly hit me.

Until that moment I hadn't thought of composing, so at the weekend I went home to Cedar Cottage on my moped, which had to be pedalled most of the way. There nineteen years of pent-up emotions erupted over a period of forty-eight hours. Luckily the masterpiece was saved and I produce it as evidence, if only to encourage others and to convince the Spirits around us that an attempt is far better than no attempt at all.

'Order! Silence in Court,' banged the Hippo Man with a broad grin on his face. 'The Defendant has said something and has brought us to observe his music at last. It is now our task to set aside our personal feelings about him and ask ourselves, in the name of grain, if he be Guilty or Not Guilty in the Eyes of Eternity.'

The Hippo Man then leant forward and received the evidence, holding it up in the air for all the Court to witness as he drew in another huge and long puff of satisfaction upon his pot-pipe. Luckily the Witch Doctors were prevented from touching the masterpiece so it has remained without a single tobacco stain.

The original manuscript is written in red biro with ruled lines because, at the time, the Defendant didn't know where to find any music paper and couldn't co-ordinate the sounds in his head with the signs on the paper.

It is, therefore, the saddest Potato you ever did see.

*Defence Exhibit One – First Composition, 1960*

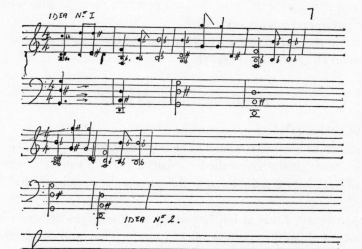

Everything about Defence Exhibit One is true, for it represents an apocalyptical musical being, if there is such a thing, whose soul has definitely developed far beyond the hills. Had the creator, who is now proud of it, submitted the work at the time to the British Broadcasting Corporation's Reading Panel (for all new compositions have to be examined by a Panel before they are either accepted or rejected for

43

broadcasting – usually rejected) I think it might have been thrown away in the wastepaper basket by mistake. But for the benefit of those Members of the Jury, Elders and Witch Doctors who cannot read music, a few basic errors, which I hope are already amusing those who can read music, ought to be pointed out.

First of all there are supposed to be four beats in a bar. Bar One, however, has three beats – Bar Two has three and a half beats – Bar Three has four and a half beats, likewise Bar Four – and poor old Bar Five has only one beat and a few arrows etc. What *we* in the West call 'Flats and Sharps' appear to be written *after* the notes instead of before them and any doctor of music will tell you that *the child* who wrote it 'doesn't even know what *key* it's in!'

You will also perceive with sorrow that the Defendant 'dried up' for there is no IDEA NO. 2 – Potato!

## Potato in No Man's Land

*A divertissement of ridiculous proportions*
The first time I went to No Man's Land was in 1962.

One could hardly have called it a jail, for it was simply a concrete cell half-way between Gibraltar and Spain, in the middle of No Man's Land.

Aged twenty, I was at last beginning to show signs of becoming a composer and had just completed a 'Suite for Flute and Piano' before departing on a memorable Spanish holiday with old Camberley friends, Jeremy Roberts and others, in a Dormobile. I shall, therefore, come back to music, the Baroness and 'being a composer' in the next bit.

Now Jeremy Roberts and the others had decided that they would drive to Gibraltar from Fuengirola, near Malaga in Spain where we were staying with a couple of 'nice ladies' who were running a villa for their friends. So we all set off for the Spanish frontier where Jeremy shattered me by asking us to hand up our passports.

'PASSPORTS!' I exclaimed. 'WE don't need passports to get into Gibraltar, we're BRITISH!'

In my ignorance, of course, I had left my passport at the villa in Fuengirola. No one seemed to care two hoots at the Spanish frontier – so on we went deeper and deeper into No Man's Land.

In case you're wondering what 'No Man's Land' is, your Courtship, it's a piece of isolated territory between two tribes which neither side care very much about as it doesn't contain any water wells or grazing grounds.

At the Gibraltar frontier, however, it was a very different story, as Jeremy had so knowledgeably pointed out. There we were confronted by a surprisingly English-looking policeman who counted all our passports and found that one was missing.

'See you at the Spanish frontier at six o'clock tonight and don't be late!' laughed the pompous Roberts who drove off leaving me stranded at the feet of polished boots.

Members of the Jury, I had brought my camera and realized I was at the time the closest I might ever get to Africa.

Almost in Africa; if it hadn't been for a sea mist, I might have even seen Africa. So I escaped, like a cattle raider, down to the Mediterranean in No Man's Land to photograph the sea, the sand, and an unusual view of the Rock of Gibraltar when suddenly I became conscious of the dull thud of heavy boots coming up behind me.

'SEÑOR! SEÑOR!'

In haste I took one last 'shot' of the Rock at a 500th of a second.

'SEÑOR!' An armed guard approached but I pretended not to see him.

'You take photograph of MEELITARY INSTALLATIONS – YOU SPY!'

'Good morning,' I said, standing to attention. 'I'm here, because I'm here, because I've left my passport at Fuengirola. I'm a tourist.'

'MEELITARY INSTALLATIONS – LOOK!' and he pointed at what I genuinely thought was a sand dune.

'YOU comey wid ME – YOU SPY!'

Together the two of us tramped back across No Man's Land, a fascinating strip of arid desert without any wells or pasture, until we

45

reached a small concrete cell near the Bay of Algeciras. It had a wooden door, this I remember well, as he promptly went and locked it – making sure that I was inside, and he outside.

It's always a ghastly feeling when you get locked up, as some of us present well know. One cannot help wondering if one will ever get out. Your Courtship – hours went by as I dripped in the stench of the cell like a rhinoceros – no one came.

Then, towards evening, I heard distant voices and more heavy boots thumping across No Man's Land. The wooden door was unlocked and there, standing before me, were two officials – one obviously more senior than the other.

'Who are you and where is your passport?' they asked.

Now, not wishing to go into the whole story again, I simply informed them that my passport was in Fuengirola where I had been staying.

'NO PASSPORT – NO SPAIN!' said The Chief.

'No passport, no Gibraltar,' I hastened to add. What a ridiculous situation to find oneself in, unable to go anywhere at all except No Man's Land, where there were no wells and no pasture.

We looked at each other and continued to look at each other for a very long time indeed, but the situation was getting quite obviously hopeless. Then, after another long look at each other, it seemed as if a brilliant idea had suddenly penetrated the skulls of my captors, for they burst into a flood of unintelligible language accompanied by wild and dangerous gesticulations. Perhaps they wanted to smuggle me out under cover of darkness, or set me free in a boat to row across the Bay of Biscay. Whatever it was it took an awful long time for them to decide before The Chief spoke again, this time in clear and simple English.

'Señor, have you any other means of identification?' he asked.

Now why the hell he hadn't thought of that in the first place I'll never know, because quite by accident I happened to have in my trouser pocket, not a pistol, but my Kensington Library Reader's Ticket which I produced as if it were evidence of the utmost importance, which it certainly is in Kensington.

'Of course, of course, this is my other means of identification, it's my BBC Union Card and it also says that I am a VERY IMPORTANT PERSON – look.'

Whereupon I turned the card over and placing my thumb over some small letters, I pointed to the words: 'VERY IMPORTANT PLEASE NOTE . . .', hoping The Chief wouldn't notice that 'Books' had to be returned within a fortnight to Kensington Public Library. Then revealing the other side of the card as if I had the power of a Witch Doctor, I pointed to my own handwriting which informed the Chief exactly who I was and where I had come from – David Fanshawe, 14 Silchester Road, London W.10 (which was at the time the Third Movement in the 'Suite of Digs').

Need I say more?

The three of us stumped back across No Man's Land exchanging views on the possibilities of developing La Linea as a tourist resort.

'Yes, of course the BBC would be interested!' I kept repeating over and over again until I was finally freed and over the border back into Spain. But I missed my lift to Fuengirola.

As for the Kensington Library Reader's Ticket? Well, I don't read books except for the Map of Africa and *Winnie-the-Pooh*, but they do have an exceptionally good record department in which I hope, one day, you will find Fanshawe's Epistles and Records as well as Bartok String Quartets!

## Your Mistakes Stretch from Here to Abyssinia

How does one become a Composer? Most budding composers seem to know they are BUDDING at the age of nine or ten. It is rare, however, to find a NON BUD, trying to BUD at the age of twenty-one. Now there are those who do POP and those who do whatever you like to call Modern Music; but the POP BUDS don't necessarily have to write theirs down any more than the Africans. They just do it – and that, in my opinion, is often much more spontaneous and uninhibited.

I point this out because, without knowing it, my bud didn't try to bud until I was shown HOW by the Baroness and later, a much longer and more developed HOW by the Royal College of Music. Nothing ever came easily to me and I doubt if it ever will. So when I played my first attempts at composition to the Baroness she remarked and I remember her words quite clearly: 'David, at last I can see where you're going. You are going to be a composer but it's going to take you years. You know nothing; you're so naïve, but you have a streak of genius.'

The Baroness then went on to question me about the 'Tonic' of F major; which is of course, the note *we* call F, but unfortunately, the only tonic I knew about was a drink you mixed with gin.

'David you are so naïve,' the Baroness kept saying.

In other words, I was just another budding Potato who didn't know how to bud.

When finally *Jill*, the piano piece, was written down and submitted to the North London Music Festival under the pseudonym 'Perstow', my old school motto, which I think means 'I stand foremost', the adjudicator asked:

'Is there anyone here called Perstow?'

'I am Perstow,' I replied standing up in front of a whole lot of other would-be buds.

'Then Perstow would you come and play me your piece which I find to be of interest.'

Perstow, hoping not to be too disgraced and knowing that his piano playing was far better than his composing, sat down at an upright piano, in a room which had too much echo, and proceeded to give a rendition of his piece.

'Is *that* how it's supposed to sound?' asked a somewhat baffled adjudicator. 'If I'd known it was going to sound like that, I might have awarded you the First Prize, but instead you will have to make do with the Second, because your mistakes stretch from here to Abyssinia.' He continued, 'You must go away and learn a technique – all you need is technique so come back and see me when you've got one.'

Unfortunately I rang the adjudicator up only the other day to see if

Standing on a 'Chic Weed' gazing out to sea

The puppets

The happy clan of
puppeteers

Stowe – the south front

The Brother used to play the flute

Male model at Canterbury Art School!

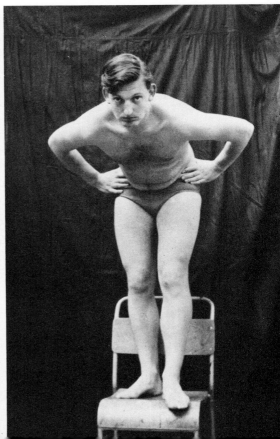

My studio at Bourne Tap where The Parents live
Judith, David, Grandpa aged 96, The Brother and the Mouse

The Father                    The Brother

Baroness Guirne van Zuylen

John Lambert

David in Hadandua tribal clothes

he could remember me, but the person on the other end of the line said that he had died.

How very sad, I thought, there's another valuable Potato gone.

S O.

Gripped with the emotions of 'being a genius' and led on by an ever-persuasive Baroness, it gradually became clearer that she was right – that I should give up my career as a film editor and take up music.

The Brother again has something to say from his ship floating about on the high seas – so prepare ye the way of the Lord!

'I never really associated the bashings on the piano at Cedar Cottage with anything to do with composition, or on occasions with music at all. My musical ear was trained to choral and classical music and I always considered that my contemporaries at St George's [Do you remember St George's?] could play the piano far better than The Brother. [Insult] This was probably not entirely true, as when he actually sat down and learnt a piece off by heart he could play it to a high standard of technical perfection. [Technical, technical, that's all they ever DO in the Navy!] I was still at St George's when the first pieces of manuscript started to appear around the piano. That is an important phrase – as I shall always think of David, composition and the piano together. [Cods-Wallop] I used to be asked what my feelings were about his latest piece. [Lovely] Nine times out of ten I would be as non-commital as possible and there seemed to be a long time when nothing was achieved at all. [Rrrrubbisssh]

His job in films brought in enough cash to get him home at weekends but I never firmly believed that he would actually leave the security of a job he liked doing for something that he didn't seem very good at. [The Navy's not always right you know!] However, we the family never gave up hope and we always told him what we thought. [You 'orrible snotty!]

I can remember the excitement as my record of Russ Conway's *Pixilated Penguin* was substituted by a very scratchy demo-disc of early Fanshawe.* There would be an argument over the volume – there still

---

* Try listening to 'Fanshawe's Early Potato Musicks' for fl, ob, cl, horn, trpt, violin, cello, percussion and 2 pianos!

is. [There still ought to be, ye guns 'ave made ye deaf!] But had it not been for the ever patient nurturing of The Mouse, I think that The Other Brother might well have ended up in some profession far re-moved from the musical world – who knows, it might have even been the Navy! [NEVER]'

## The Line to Clapman Omon

'Bwana! Bwana Chief!' interrupted the Municipal Armory, who addressed a somewhat sudden plea for attention to the Hippo Man. 'The telephone is ringing now and we think it's the Outside World who wants to speak to us. Have we permission to answer them?'

'Answer them,' ordered the Hippo Man.

The Municipal Armory answered the telephone and the Defendant instantly recognized the familiar voice of his old friend, Annette Battams, who must have been speaking from Clapham Common.

Annette (Netty) and her husband Leo Aylen, both dynamic person-alities, have definitely budded. Netty is a composer and singer, and Leo an author and poet of distinction, who at the time of the Trial is a Poet in Residence in America.

'Jambo! Jambo!' said the voice from the Outside World which resounded round the courtroom, a typical 'Netty voice' if you can imagine it for a moment.

'Netty!' shouted the Defendant. 'For God's sake help! I'm in the middle of nowhere on the Hill of Eternity and I'm on trial. Can you tell the Hippo Man and all the others what I was like when you first met me in 1964? . . . Netty listen . . . I'm trying to tell the Hippo Man, Elders and Witch Doctors about myself before I went to the Royal College of Music . . . I'm trying to write a book, but I don't read books except for the Map of Africa and *Winnie-the-Pooh* . . .'

'HARAMBEE!' came a monstrously naughty-sounding reply from Clapham Common as the line was held up over the heads of the magnificently plumed Witch Doctors so that everybody could hear better.

'ORDER!' barked the Hippo Man. 'We must all work together and pay attention to the Outside World – Harambee! Where did you say it was?'

'Clapman Omon,' replied the Municipal Armory. 'And we can only just hear it. Pray for rain, green grass and for silence, because the line is bad.' The Hippo Man then stretched forward across a huge desk, which had been lent to him by the Headmaster of the Secondary School of the Sacred Heart at the bottom of the Hill of Eternity. Snatching hold of the line, which was attached to the lower branches of an Elephant Tree, the Hippo Man and the rest of the Court listened with astonishment to the disembodied voice of the Outside World.

'Jambo!' said the voice again.

'Jambo sana!' replied the Court in a deep, humorous sort of chorus, surprised that the line produced a sound they could all understand.

'Jambo! Jambo!' repeated the voice of the Outside World, enjoying every moment of its repeat.

'Jambo! Jambo sana!' replied the Court, not knowing if the voice was a Bwana or a Bibi (Mrs).

'Can I speak in English? Or would it be better in French?' squawked Netty.

'Just speak,' said the Defendant, who feared the line would get cut off before anything had been said at all.

Netty's voice continued: ' . . I remember being thunderstruck by David's sheer power and physical presence. He once said to me with great passion – "I want to find GOD". He stressed God very heavily as if there was no God in his music at that time. It had no spine, no reason for being there. He seemed to be thrashing about like a fish out of water. I remember he told me how much he admired French composers and wanted to emulate their sense of style and craftsmanship . . .' [It's funny how most composers go through the 'French period!']

'It was these statements which prompted me to introduce him to John Lambert – a man so utterly different from himself. I felt that John's esoteric qualities, coupled with his sense of refinement and extreme sophistication, might become a part of David's extraordinary, half-peasant, middle-class, total-primitive, naïve and simple make-up. I felt that he would be the right teacher for David and I knew John would be interested . . .'

With those prophetic words the Hill of Eternity's line of communication, transmitted via the satellite station in the Rift Valley, was suddenly cut off. It was as if the Outside World no longer existed.

The Municipal Armory hung up their end of the line on the lower branches of the Elephant Tree, which was immediately blessed in a special ceremony by the Court who encircled the tree and repeated an impromptu blessing. The Defendant's guide from the School of the Sacred Heart translated it into English:

> God bless this, the tree of Clapman Omon.
> God bless our tree, the tree of Clapman Omon.
> God save our tree, the tree of the Outside World.

The Defendant then thanked the Court for having listened to the voice of a lifelong friend and asked the Hippo Man if he could read out a tribute he had written to John Lambert, who was to become his next music professor for several years. The Baroness had decided to go and live in France.

The Court settled down again into their former positions of satisfaction. It was at last getting cooler. Slowly, beautiful peace descended upon them as the African sun sank and settled into the lands of Bush and Glory below the Hill of Eternity.

The Defendant, perched on a small, round, locally carved wooden stool with three legs, then began to pay his respects. First of all to those present and then to all those who had recently joined the scene of the Trial. Finally he read out his tribute to John Lambert. Everybody listened in silence as the birds sang above them in the branches of the Elephant Tree in the evening cool. It was almost dark as women prepared more beer in a hut to one side of the Court, for the celebrations would undoubtedly continue throughout the night, until the dawn of the next day.

### *John Lambert*

In a nutshell John *is* John!
If I were a Poet I would write a Poem about him.
If I were a Clown I would laugh with him.
If I were a Tenor, or an Alto, or a Bass,
or even a Soprano worth my salt,
I would know him intimately.

For I would say he is *the study* of my voice,
For John can *hear* me singing.
John can *look in* and understand what I am trying
    to do,
And what I am trying to say.
John knows.
He *has* been, and always *will* be my teacher
whatever the weather is doing outside.

John taught me how to reason;
How to be myself;
How to explore and expand in the way that I
    wanted to;
How to harness my invention;
How to discipline my craft.
He was a sympathetic ear and he heard me calling
when I really needed him.

And now I have introduced you to John.
John Lambert, Composer, Teacher and Friend.

## Initiation into the Royal College of Music

*Cap in hando*
Members of the Jury, I had to have T W O interviews.

    The first, it seemed, went reasonably well until I was called down for the very unexpected second interview. If only the ways of the College had been known to me then as they are now I would have understood that a second interview did not mean one was being looked at as a potential reject, but that one had passed the Entrance Exam with flying colours and was being sent down to the Director as a possible candidate for a Foundation Scholarship. I automatically assumed they were having one last look at me to see if there was anything they could salvage before throwing me out as a rejected Potato. It was at the second interview that I had the good fortune to meet Sir Keith Falkner, the Director, and Dr Gordon Jacob, for the first time.

Firmly convinced of my failure, I told them exactly of my plight – and what a plight it was!

'I very much want to come to the College to study composition with John Lambert,' I said. 'If you accept me, I shall then have a good chance of getting a County Grant and won't have to go on working as a part-time male model in Canterbury Art School. If I don't get into College I shall continue my studies privately with Mr Lambert but will waste a lot of time being a male model, hitch-hiking up and down to London for my music lessons.'

Dr Jacob at this point looked up, quite speechless and dropped his glasses on the desk.

'You what?' he said.

'Male model for life classes at Canterbury Art School,' I replied (see photograph), and proceeded to give the distinguished company a demonstration of what I did for a living. In fact, I nearly decided to take my trousers off there and then, knowing full well what my fate was going to be, but instead I spoke of my fears at having to take the 'written paper' in the afternoon. We talked for a short while and then they asked me to play another of my piano pieces which only looked impressive because it happened to be published.

'Are you sure you want to come here?' asked Sir Keith.

'Quite sure,' I replied, and then went on to apologize saying that I would be incapable of doing *any* Harmony and Theory without the aid of a piano and therefore didn't think I could take the Theory paper at all. So wishing them a 'good morning' I slipped out of the door.

54

In the afternoon, as expected, the examination hall was filled with what appeared to be some three hundred budding geniuses, for as soon as the word had been given to GO they buried their heads in reams of manuscript paper and confidently poured out their horrid little brains with horrific rapidity – nobody used a piano!

I stared at a blank sheet of paper for a very long time and then stuck up my hand. At last the examiner saw it and treading very carefully between the rows of College desks ('Tiptoe through the College') he approached me.

'I'm terribly sorry,' I whispered, 'I cannot answer any of these questions.'

'Then why do you want to come to the Royal College?' he asked in very hushed tones.

'Could you please give me the easier paper?' I urged, 'because I am a composer and cannot do the composer's "Special Paper" with all these questions about String Quartets in the style of Haydn. I haven't heard *any* Quartets by Haydn.'

The examiner, who seemed shocked by what had just been admitted, went away again, tiptoeing through the College desks which he needn't have done as there was such a terrible racket going on in the road outside; an electrical drill let off relentless fortissimos – BRRRRRrrrr!... BBBBBBrrrr!... BRRRRRrrrr! Hardly conducive to musical enterprise, but then one always had to put up with a terrible racket going on in College.

When the examiner returned, tiptoeing all the way back again shaking his head, I solemnly handed him a blank sheet of paper at the bottom of which was written a desperate message:

N.B. I'M SORRY I HAVE WASTED YOUR TIME.

Very despondently, Fanshawe hitch-hiked home to Kent, down the A20, knowing full well that he had failed. The Family had by this time moved to the smugglers' cottage called Bourne Tap. In the depths of despair, he said to The Mouse:

'It's no good, I've failed. I couldn't do the Harmony Paper and had to have *two* interviews – the whole thing was a disaster. I'm *not* a musician after all.'

Forty-eight hours later, however, nothing short of a miracle happened. There I was fast asleep in my pit in the studio in the garden, when I became conscious of The Father's voice, which sounded terribly severe.

'David,' he called out. 'You'd better come up, there's a letter for you from the Royal College.'

Oh God, I thought, feeling sick in the stomach at the very thought of it and what it would mean. Dragging myself up the path under the apple tree past Grandpa's Cabin and up the stairs to The Tap, I met the most anxious looking father you ever saw. To make things worse he had a streaming cold.

The letter was handed to me. I opened it, read it – then read it again, and again – and then handed it to The Father who said, 'They *must* have made a mistake, I'll ring them up . . .'

The Mouse read it and shouted out loud – her bosom swelling with pride – 'HOOOoooorrRRRAAY! We ARE a musician after all!'

Even Grandpa saw it – 'CONGRATULATIONS!' he said, which is what he always says if anyone does anything good.

The reply from the College was printed in red with my name written on it in ink, and after The Father had rung them up we all heaved a sigh of relief because the following information had been confirmed with the College Registrar, John R. Stainer, O.B.E.:

### SCHOLARSHIPS 1965

Mr   *David Arthur Fanshawe*

I am pleased to inform you that you have been awarded   *Foundation Scholarship*

tenable at the College, from September next.

Since then I have often been asked if my family are musical. The answer is YES in one sense and NO in another. As you can see I was hardly brought up within the 'Socio-Musico-Worldio' if you know what I mean.

Our Father sings the bass line in Bilsington Church quite naturally, whereas I sing the bass line quite unnaturally. The Brother *used* to play the flute and once upon a time sang treble, but we at home never heard it, even when he was Head Chorister at St George's. Grandpa (ninety-six) in his quiet way is perhaps the most musical of us all for he still listens to concerts on his 'Wireless' down in his 'Cabin' after weeding. Grandpa's concerts are usually played very loud and I'm sure he would like me to 'congratulate' the BBC on his behalf for their services. As for The Mouse she can always spot a good tune, but when she tries to sing in Church – nothing comes out at all!

The Grannies, who are now in heaven with Grandfather Fan, both 'adored' music. Granny Fan used to play the violin rather well and led a frightfully keen orchestra for the SIMLA A.D.S. (Simla Amateur Dramatic Society) of which Grandfather Fan was a very popular and prodigious producer. In fact Them at Home have often said that a lot of my 'Drama' comes from Grandfather Fan. Granny Mosse (Grandpa's wife) on the other hand, used to imagine all sorts of things but never really did them. Granny Mosse and I had a great affinity with each other and I've often felt that 'her kind of spirit' is leaning over my left shoulder. The Mouse says it's sometimes Granny Mosse's spirit and sometimes it's Elgar's. These days I don't think it's either!

At any rate, wherever the Grannies are I hope they are enjoying themselves as much as we used to on those picnics in the 'Bluebell Woods' near Frensham Ponds.

## Studente espressivo

As a first year student at the R.C.M. I lived with a vicar and his merry wife in a vicarage, which you might be able to find if you look hard enough, between the Oval and Brixton.

It was there that I wrote a lot of 'light' music including *Fantasy on Dover Castle* – an orchestral tone poem (rather too short) which had been inspired by a view I once had of Dover Castle from a cross-channel ferry in a force ten gale, whilst returning from Boulogne to Dover. The passengers were in a terrible state, heaving up their guts all round me, when one poor old lady – seemingly at death's door – squeaked:

'Cun yer see Dowver Carstle yut?'

Whereupon an Elgarian-type tune, and a long one at that, came into my head as we tossed and turned upon the ocean outside the entrance to Dover Harbour. It went like this . . . I am now imagining the tune and singing it to myself. If *you* want to know what it sounds like, you'd better go down to Chappell's Orchestral Hire Library and hope they can dig it out.

In many ways it sounded rather better on the piano than played by the orchestra but the vicar's wife (Fourth Movement in the 'Suite of Digs') said: 'If you go on writing music like that you'll be another GREAT ENGLISH COMPOSER and God knows we could do with a few more of them.' She said – she kept saying.

However, it seemed all her high hopes were dashed to the ground when I began to wail in Arabic; the result was that the vicar failed to become a Muslim and merely informed me one evening that I should have to leave the vicarage. In other words, I was sacked because they not only objected to my musical development but to my social behaviour as well since I *was* rather inclined to get up in the afternoon when not on parade at the College.

Fanshawe and his music moved to Addison Road, which is at the bottom of Kensington High Street, to the house of the industrious Mrs Medlam who put up with an awful lot and earned herself the title – Fifth Movement in the 'Suite of Digs'.

Meanwhile, back at the College, one had to fulfil certain College obligations, such as attending choral class, in other words singing in the choir; attending lectures which included Antony Hopkins's 'Music as an Art and Science' and Dr Philip Wilkinson's 'The History of Music'. Both series I found most enjoyable and they always had a large and appreciative turnout. More than that, College life was what *you* made of it and what you were prepared to put into it. Some put into it more than others.

Every student was required to take two main subjects. Mine were

Composition first, including Harmony and Theory (all with John Lambert) and Conducting second. But in five years at the College I never took an exam, as I knew 'an exam' would be of NO use to me whatsoever and I had no intention of teaching because no authority would stick me. The College Authorities were most co-operative and very liberal-minded on general points of this nature according to the *individual concerned*.

With me – I don't think they knew quite what to think!

# III

# *Journey to the Holy Land, 1966*

Members of the Jury and Greater Public, it all sounds a bit fantastical, I know, but at the end of a year of it, in the summer vacation of 1966, having hitch-hiked all over Europe and then having completed a year at the College, I became utterly obsessed with the idea of exploring, more thoroughly this time, the Middle East. My aim was to see the Holy Land. To experience it at first hand and hopefully to lose myself in the deserts of Southern Jordan and Arabia, reading the Bible as I went.

I counted myself an experienced hitch-hiker (semi-professional) and on this, my first expedition to the Middle East, I established a method of getting there by rule of thumb and commando-like tactics in under ten days. The magical route was as follows:

Dover to Ostende, Ostende to Aachen, Aachen to Munich, Munich to Zagreb, Zagreb to Belgrade, Belgrade to Sofia, Sofia to the motel at Plovdiv (where I always allowed myself at least a dinner and a decent bed), Plovdiv to Istanbul, Istanbul to Ankara and on this, the Holy Land expedition, from Ankara to Damascus, to Amman and then to hospital! For the first lesson I learnt in the Middle East was that one couldn't really fool around with the heat unless one wore some kind of a sun-protector on one's head. Nowadays I wear what has become a rather well-known woolly cap. But in those days I liked to imagine myself as some kind of Lawrence of Arabia.

At Muasher Hospital in Amman I was said to be suffering from exhaustion and dehydration. Can you wonder – the journey only took six days.

Now I've no desire to dwell too much on the Holy Land journeys, I only want to point out to you, Members of the Jury, that it stimulated in me a far deeper desire to Travel and Explore. One doesn't just become a good traveller. Travelling is knowing WHAT to see, HOW to see it and much more important WHEN TO RECORD what one sees as accurately as one can. I believe that this is a talent which can only be developed from humble beginnings and you couldn't imagine anything more humble than this.

Having risen from my pit in Muasher Hospital I hitched down to Aqaba on the Red Sea having heard about a fantastic wadi (valley) which lay somewhere to the East in the shimmering sands of the 'Mountains of the Moon'. Having failed to find a guide who would take me there on a camel I went in search of a gregarious Arab by the name of Zuhair Mograby, an alleged champion swimmer, redeveloper, friend of the King and ship's chandler. It took me a long time to find him and when I did, like so many other promises made in the Middle East, Zuhair *promised* to take me to Wadi Ram but the very next day, when I returned in the stifling heat, his sister merely informed me that her brother had gone to the Lebanon where he was said to be 'very busy'.

Exhausted, since it was physically painful to walk a hundred yards in that heat, I collapsed on the golden sands of the Red Sea and by good fortune met two other English boys who needed little persuasion when I told them about Wadi Ram. The three of us at last set off in a hired Land-Rover.

The driver spoke a little English and when I asked him whether he had heard of Lawrence of Arabia, for he seemed quite elderly – his eyes lit up, the Land-Rover swerved all over the place and with tremendous passion, he shouted, his turban flying in the wind:

'EL'ORANCE, EL'ORANCE I NO DIS MUN, HE VERY FUNNY FELLO...I NO AS I WUS DI TRRRUCK DRRRIVER...HE PETER OH'TOOL – HE AND DAVEEED LEEEN...VERY FUNNY FELLO!'

Upon the final words of this recitation which he repeated over and over again, we suddenly careered off into the red sand of the desert and by evening were surrounded by the huge towering rock faces of the wadi and the little fortress of Ram.

'Here it is!' I thought and simply couldn't believe it, it was SO fantastic – THE DESERT!

Very quickly the pink glow of evening became the silent stillness of night and we slept under the walls of the fortress with a Jordanian police patrol and their camels.

SLEEP? Of course I couldn't sleep. The whole sky twinkled far too brilliantly. Then there came that moment in the desert, which on subsequent journeys I became so familiar with – the moment when the desert begins to stir. Camels are watered, goats milked and sent out to graze and there is the unbelievable beauty of dawn and strange noises which no words can express. Already in the distance I watched as a line of camels humped along under the towering rocks.

Our Trrruck Drrriver, however, appeared to be utterly unmoved by the very obvious physical and emotional tenderness which so many of us feel when at last we find the desert. I have so often discovered this to be true in Africa and Arabia for we as human beings are never content with what we have, we always seem to crave for what we have not. So often this happens, as it did on that particular morning when my 'whole being' awoke to the call of the desert. There I was, standing still in time and space surrounded by huge granite blocks of stone rising sheer from the desert floor. The sun came up and everything was transformed into a glorious redness which fired my imagination into believing that the desert and its grandeur could take on the expression of new musical forms. I suddenly became acutely aware of my creativity and felt that it might be able to expand, just as my vision was being expanded and stretched to a far wider horizon in the desert than I had ever imagined.

The desert is alive – not dead, and at some times of the year it becomes a botanical paradise, every Bedouin will tell you that; but our truck driver on that particular morning simply couldn't understand why anybody should want to go back to Aqaba on a camel when he had at his disposal, not only a Land-Rover, but a 'Drrriver' who had 'drriven El'Orance'.

Both he and the Land-Rover were *deeply* insulted. A cloud of red dust shot up into the sky as he drove off indignantly shouting and gesticulating to Allah:

'EL'ORANCE, EL'ORANCE I NO DIS MUN, HE VERY FUNNY

FELLO...I NO AS I WUS DI TRRRUCK DRRRIVER...HE PETER
OH'TOOL – HE AND DAVEEED LEEEN...VERY FUNNY FELLO!
EL'ORANCE, EL'ORANCE...'

Finally, when I came out of the desert and was sitting on my pack on
the tarmac road waiting for a lift from Aqaba to Amman, I wrote: 'I
have seen a great sight in the name of the Lord; WADI RAM.'

The Parents must have thought this sentence rather odd as I failed to
explain who or what Wadi Ram actually was. When eventually a lift
did come, I lay in the back of the vehicle and wept bitterly, hoping no
one would see me, as the desert had stirred up my deepest emotions.

## In the Valley of the Shadow of Death

From Amman I hitched a ride to Jerusalem and having stayed in the
Old City for a few days decided to go out into the wilderness of Judaea.
So climbing the Mount of Olives I walked due east, again with a pack
on my back and a loaf of bread. My objective was the River Jordan. It
was one of those walks one never forgets. In the evening of the first
day I came upon a deep gorge in the wilderness.

'Surely this must be the Valley of the Shadow of Death?' I thought
as I descended into the gorge following the spiral tracks of sheep and
goats which scarred the barren landscape. In Jerusalem some French
archaeologists had told me about 'the Valley' saying that if I continued
to walk across the wilderness in a certain direction, keeping the Mount
of Temptation on my left, I was bound to discover it. They were right.

At the bottom of the gorge there was a beautiful spring and much to
the amusement of some shepherds, I lay down and drank huge gulps
like some character out of a Hollywood movie. I also ate bread and wild
berries.

The following morning I read the Bible and continued to walk down
the Valley of the Shadow of Death. The archaeologists had also told me
that the gorge got its legendary name from the days when armies used
to be ambushed while attempting to cut through the wilderness from
Jericho to Jerusalem. It was an extraordinary sight. The gorge contained

hundreds of caves in which there still live many hermits. One could quite easily imagine how it became known as the Valley of the Shadow of Death.

On the second evening I became ill and lost a lot of fluid. I also suffered from a fearful buzzing in the head. In the morning, quite by accident, I came upon a tiny Greek Orthodox monastery suspended on the side of a precipice. Looking up I saw some old priests leaning over a balcony. They had long, white beards – Prophets from the Old Testament?

It was there at the monastery I was able to rest for three days and read the Bible. The incident later became the subject of my first *accepted* broadcast on BBC Radio – a scripted talk for 'Woman's Hour' called 'Alone in the Wilderness' which lasted four and a half minutes!

Members of the Jury, I don't know if any of this is of interest, but I put it to you in three words: EVERYTHING SEEMS RELEVANT.

Out of the Valley of the Shadow of Death I came, looking like a wild man from the hills, and having reached Jericho, went on to the Traditional Baptismal Site on the banks of the River Jordan. The following incident, which I will relate to you word for word as I remember it, is the truth, the whole truth and nothing but the truth.

## Fanshawe Baptizes Americans in Jordan

Minding my own business, and nobody else's, I was standing up to my neck in the waters of Jordan taking photographs of the surroundings with my old Paxette camera, when up swirled three bus loads of American tourists from Jerusalem. Seeing me in the river the leader, whose name was George, shouted out:

'HEY! There's a man in the wader, HEY WHAT'S YER NAME?'

'DAVID,' I replied, a little ashamed of the Fanshawe part.

'HEY! We gat DAVID in the River Jordan here, he can Baptize the people.'

'But I'm not a priest,' I explained.

'Oh, that don't matter, anybudy can Baptize us, we're from Southern

Georgia,' said George as he produced a blue plastic bottle, 'and you really gat yer feet wet haven't you.'

'But what do I do?' I asked.

'Yer fill up the bwottle with the Holy Water and then you put yer arm around the person's waist and placing yer–uther arm on the person's heayrd you say,' and at this point George spoke as if he were trying to break the world speech record:

'I Baptize-Thee-in-the-Name-of-the-Father-the-Son-and-the-Holy-Ghost – Aymean.'

'Is that all?' I asked. 'Can anybody do that?'

'Well you be Christian don'tee?' he exclaimed.

By this time about eighty Americans were already eagerly filling up their plastic 'bwottles' and some were finding it a bit difficult as the banks of the river at the Traditional Baptismal Site were rather steep and muddy.

'This is definitely going to be a long job,' I thought to myself.

Then, at about four o'clock, having baptized about thirty of them, I remember one good lady in particular who was wearing a flowered dress with a large hat which seemed to have a strawberry 'fruit salad' on the top of it. This she refused to remove and when it came to her turn she became positively hysterical shouting out to George:

'Hey, GEORGE! Wat's the time?'

'Oh, shut-up-about-the-time-Elsie. Just yer git yerself Baptized and PRAY to the Good Lord.' George hovered on the brink waving a camera in our direction which had an enormous lens on it.

'Gee I'm scared, I cayn't git down there George! Help me David, so help me Gard!' screamed Elsie.

So offering Elsie two sturdy, bronzed arms, I helped and persuaded her into the water. (Members of the Jury, by this time I was sinking fast.)

'Have you gat hold of me David, I'm so scared and Ay can't be Baptized till's FUR o'clark, 'cos Maryee-back-home is thinkin' and prayin' fer me – hey George is it FUR O'CLARK YET?'

George didn't have time to answer as he was far too busy manipulating his expensive camera, still trying to point it in the right direction.

Slowly I raised my right arm out of Jordan and upon Elsie's strawberry hat I delivered the Holy Waters saying, in a very English voice of course:

'I Baptize Thee in the Name of the Father, and of the Son, and of the Holy Ghost, A . . .'

'Did-yer-git-the-picture-George?' screeched Elsie, smothering the 'Amen' as we both began to disappear under the Holy Waters; at which point a party of Nuns drifted by in a boat singing Hymns to the Good Lord.

Elsie struggled all over the place as I tried to fill up 'hers' and 'Maryee-back-home's' bwottle after she had insisted that both bwottles be filled from the middle of the river, which wasn't at all easy because the Holiest part of Jordan was very deep and had a very strong current.

George, however, came to the rescue and managed to heave Elsie out – but Fanshawe, unfortunately, was seen to be drifting quite helplessly downstream waving both bwottles in the air to the strains of the Nuns singing in the boat 'Praise to the holiest in the height and in the depths be praise . . .'

## Musical Thoughts in Jerusalem

*Momento serioso*

On returning to Jerusalem I stayed once again in a little hotel in the heart of the Old City and every morning I remember the deep and sonorous tones of an Imam who stirred the faithful to prayer:

'Allahu Akber, Allahu Akber.' God is great, God is great.

It was there, lying in a drowsy, half-conscious state, that I first became aware of the Muslim 'Call to Prayer' and the sounds of the faithful reciting the Quran in the Mosque – those strange and beautiful melodic lines.

One day, I went to a service at St George's Cathedral in Jerusalem and as the choir sang, I heard from the City outside 'those other recitations' blending in from the Mosques all around. It was such a peaceful harmony, a natural Symphony of Man glorifying his Creator – for there is only ONE Creator I am sure.

With an inward longing for peace and harmony and with the sudden realization that Muslims and Christians were praying at the same time within earshot of each other, a new seed was sown from which future compositions would rise.

## Israel

Your Courtship, I am simply a composer who loves the world and the people who live in it. If I had my way there would be no borders, for there should be no borders – just as the Land follows the Sea.

Time was running short and I was determined to see as much of Israel as I could before returning to the College; I would like to quote from two letters which were written to The Parents, the first dated 30 August 1966:

'Dear to The Mouse and to The Father and to all the others,

This is written by me, without. Here I am in a shirt that's dripping sweat in a fan-cooled café in Tel Aviv. Four days ago I returned from a disastrous hike a thousand miles all over the Negev Desert only to find that again my camera shutter had jammed. You can imagine my state – all the film completely wasted. However, at reasonable cost I have now hired another camera and am about to repeat the entire expedition all over again.

What an interesting and varied country Israel is. I have today come back from an expedition to Galilee, Nazareth, Cana, Capernaum and Deganya where I stayed in one of the oldest Kibbutz in the country. This was most interesting but definitely not for me as you have to do everything in accordance with your fellow "Kibbutzniks!" I was told off several times for photographing puddles and for trying to get up a tower to photograph the valley. However, I have taken pictures of the moon rising over the Syrian Mountains and the golden corn in the sunset looking down on the Sea of Galilee. I have followed the path of

Jesus of Nazareth to the Mount of Beatitudes and have seen a strange and wonderful sight in the name of the Lord.'

Then in the second letter dated 5 September 1966 I wrote:

'. . . Two days ago I photographed a Bedouin home. Just a tent and a wife, a girl and a camel, some goats and the owner with a small black kettle. This was *his* home, a small rise on the desert floor. My home is also where I come from and where I belong. It is the home which is the life behind the man who goes out and gives what he can where he lives and belongs. It is the home which means as much to the Arab as it does to the Jew, as it does to the man from Colorado or the man from Putney.

It is now having seen, that he who writes is thinking about *his* home. For in the days to come with thousands of miles above and behind he will come from The Foreign – a little more brown and weathered with shoes that can hardly hold together for the walk. But he comes with a smile which is happy to see them again.'

## Journey Home

In some extraordinary way, I always felt something special when I returned from The Foreign. There was the feeling of distance, the feeling of travelling home across Europe to the English Channel and back to the view of the White Cliffs of Dover which reminded me of the 'Fantasy' which went like this . . . I am now imagining it and sing-ing it to myself.

Every year, hitch-hiking home from The Foreign, I would try and call in on Janette Ferguson, who lived in Rome, and another old friend I affectionately nicknamed 'The Giraffe' because she was rather tall. So we all went off to the Isle of Capri and I wrote one final 'mossage' on a postcard to Them at Home which read:

'I am sitting in a beautiful position looking out over the Bay of Naples on top of the Isle of Capri.

A wonderful sight has beheld my eye-full and I have been composing a very bad tune on an equally bad piano with the aid of some German tourists who say it's marvellous and "how nice to find a musician in such a lovely situation so many feet up in the air".

I am happy and the sun he sets.'

## Requiem for the Children of Aberfan

*Progressively contrapuntal*

Sir Keith Falkner commented in his opening address in September 1966:

'Thank you for your warm welcome. I trust we are all delighted to be back in College and ready for the new academic year . . . Since we separated for the summer vacation we have all pursued our individual ideas for a holiday; my wife and I buried ourselves in rural Suffolk and came back, like you I hope, full of energy for the New Year. The student who lived with the Bedouin in the desert, rode camels and toured Israel and Jordan thereby "acquiring a much better knowledge of the Bible" deserves special mention. I hope David Fanshawe has brought back a film of his holiday so that we may have the pleasure of seeing it in College . . .'

Pretty tough holiday!

It was wonderful, however, to be mentioned in the address and I always found, even in the darkest days when I couldn't see *where* I was going, that the College and those responsible for my musical development had tremendous faith in what I attempted to do.

Travelling had now bitten me severely – but as yet it still bore little relationship to my studies or to my compositions. John Lambert had been gently applying pressure, persuading me to get away from writing 'light music' so that I could apply my energies and expand my ideas and concepts, especially as I was now a second year student.

Then, on the tragic day when the news broke that there had been a disaster at Aberfan in Wales, everything began to 'gel'. It happened that on that very day I was travelling to Conway in North Wales with my

69

College contemporary and friend, the conductor, Owain Arwel Hughes, to organize a music course at the Holiday Fellowship Centre. On our arrival we heard about the terrible tragedy at Aberfan when one hundred and sixteen school children and several teachers died under the slag heaps which fell so suddenly on Pantglas School – the date was 21 October 1966.

The following morning many people went to Chapel and we attended a special Service of prayers in Conway for all those who were bereaved at Aberfan. The Service, almost entirely spoken in Welsh, was one of the most moving I can remember and as I stood there, with Owain beside me, I felt something mighty striking in my head and once again I was reminded of the great mountains and deserts of Wadi Ram and the mirage.

For the first time I suddenly *heard* in my head an extended musical form with three monumental outbursts from an orchestra followed by a mystical section which represented the children who had died playing happily in heaven.

In the middle of the Service the Minister beckoned a young boy, aged about eight, to join him from the congregation. The child had very blond hair. The Minister, who was very tall, put his arm around the child who recited a poem from memory in Welsh. Then there was a short silence during which the sun dramatically pierced through the windows for a moment, bathing both figures in brilliant sunlight.

It was as if they were being lifted up towards heaven and I kept hearing a strange, yet beautiful sound representing all that I had seen in the deserts of Southern Jordan, now symbolized in the tragedy which had happened only a few miles from the Chapel in which we thought and prayed.

After the boy had finished reciting, the Minister spoke again – one short sentence, the only sentence spoken in English; he said: 'Suffer the little children to come unto me, for theirs is the Kingdom of Heaven.'

At which point his voice began to break and it seemed as though he were unable to go on speaking. Gently leading the boy by the shoulder he took him back to the congregation. Then everything became blurred and I had to leave. Owain came with me.

This part of the Autobiography I find hard to write, especially as I was at last beginning to discover a way of expressing myself which developed both aspects of my turbulent nature – MUSIC and TRAVEL.

So rather than take everything that happened in its chronological order, I would like to throw you into that turbulent world, as I see this 'Book' developing in a series of gigantic steps, not unlike the waves of cacophonic sound which build up to the central climax – the three monumental outbursts in my composition *Requiem for the Children of Aberfan*.

Owain was a post-graduate student at the College studying conducting. He always had great affinity with my music and used to perform it with his own orchestra at the College. Since then, in the profession, we have collaborated many times, notably on the recording of *African Sanctus*.

*Requiem for the Children of Aberfan*, however, was first performed (its only performance to date) at an official College Concert conducted by Professor Harvey Phillips with the Second Orchestra, on the second anniversary of the tragedy in 1968. Harvey Phillips took endless trouble and I would like to thank him and the orchestra for an amazing performance which I believe will be remembered by many who heard it. Here is an extract from a review by Alison Truefitt written for *The Times Educational Supplement*:

'It is unashamed programme music. Three monumental outbursts, orchestral explosions such as one rarely hears even in these unfettered times, mark the climax of the piece. The moving mountain is heard in successive waves of cacophonic sound, sustained at the conductor's discretion until the concert hall itself seems in peril. Three gong strokes warn of the final cataclysm which subsides amid disjointed bell-ringing into one minute's silence. The ethereal image of the children playing in heaven was well captured by a tape-recorded insert of a Debussy-esque interlude for two flutes and piano; the disembodied sound expressing the children's absence. The requiem ended with desolate repetitions of a single note, D, on the piano.

It is a powerful work. Some unison string passages – expressing, perhaps, the parents' helpless grief – did not quite sustain the intensity of the rest, but there were some poignant moments in the slow, contrapuntal re-entry of the orchestra after that long silence. With the memory of the disaster still fresh in many minds, Mr Fanshawe's requiem could hardly fail to be moving . . .

If it tended to be a series of vivid, almost pictorial effects, rather than the sustained reflection of the traditional requiem, that is perhaps not inappropriate. A brutal act merits brutal treatment.'

### *Exhibit Two – Early Sketch of Requiem*

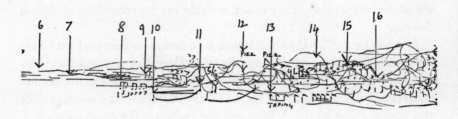

In this sketch, one of the earliest from the Requiem, you can see how the Defendant began to *draw* his music out of the landscape of his journeys. If you compare the sketch with the photograph of Wadi Ram you will also see a strong geographical resemblance.

Exhibit Three shows part of the finished manuscript and you will agree I hope, that the Defendant has come a long way from his performance in Exhibit One!

It is not necessary for you to be able to read music, just look at the manuscript as if it were a map. So much of the understanding of music depends upon its visual appearance. The full score of the Requiem was written note for note in the Defendant's own hand, using pen and ink. It took him eighteen months to complete the work.

### Exhibit Three – 'Requiem for the Children of Aberfan'

# IV

# *Journey to Iran, Bahrain and Abu Dhabi, 1967*

In order to raise enough money to hitch back to the Middle East, this time to Iran, the Persian Gulf and in particular the Island of Bahrain – where I had a notorious Uncle, Commodore Tom Fanshawe – it was necessary for me to sell the engagement ring I had bought for the Bumble's sister. At the end of my second year at the R.C.M. I thought I had fallen in love with her, but the Bumble's sister 'broke it off' which left me with the princely sum of £25 – just about enough money to get me to the sands of the Empty Quarter in Saudi Arabia. 'Bumble', a very old friend, used to hitch-hike with me on European holidays long before I ever contemplated doing any serious musical research.

So, once again The Father drove me down to Dover docks, as he had done the year before and the year before that and dropped me off at the traffic lights in front of a notice which read: NO FOOT PASSENGERS ALLOWED.

'Excuse me sir,' I said to one of the drivers queuing at the lights, 'I'm terribly sorry to bother you, but could you possible give me a lift on to the car-ferry as I want to get to Bahrain in time for my uncle's daughter's wedding on Sunday.'

What else could the poor fellow do but oblige and then apologize profusely saying that he was only going as far as Denmark! But the lift served its purpose and without further delay I was on the boat to freedom.

Once on board the procedure was simple – to ferret around for another vehicle going at least as far as the German Autobahns. So spying two elderly ladies in their elderly Austin, for they obviously had

74

an empty back seat, I started to convince them that I was 'persona'. They seemed a little startled at first, until I produced a letter of introduction written on headed College paper – very useful in emergencies – it worked a treat and the ladies promised to give me a lift in the morning to Cologne.

The next word The Parents got was on the back of a postcard from Yugoslavia two days later:

'. . . Yes indeed! Here IT is on a lovely sunny morning in the old city of Belgrade by the River Sava. Ahead of last year's hike by almost twelve hours. Leaving for Sofia at 7 a.m. two straight lifts from Yugoslav frontier and altogether nine lifts in two days from Ostende. Gloria! Here ends the news.'

You must understand I always looked smart on 'the road', usually wearing a blazer, old school tie, short hair and sometimes even a rolled umbrella!

Here are *my* essential tips for a successful hitch-hike, other hikers please take note:

a. Don't use drivers unmercifully – only use them mercifully!
b. Don't smoke and drop ash everywhere.
c. Don't sit like a pudding as if the world owes you a living – because it doesn't!
d. Never walk. Always look at your driver and communicate with him using your eyes and a firm voice.
e. Don't forget to run when he takes the trouble to stop.
f. Use the road with respect and choose your spot with care and consideration for the driver.
g. If you are a genuine hiker motivated by an interest in the Arts, People, Travel etc. and if you *really* want to achieve something in your life – good luck to you!

'Here is the news from the depths of central Turkey,' I wrote on 4 August 1967 to Them at Home:
'. . . My luck turned yet again this morning at Yozgat having spent a

very cold night in a barn full of corn. During the course of the night I nearly drowned in the corn so went and sat on a stump by the side of the road and read The Acts of the Apostles. At 6.30 a.m. out of the cold, grey mist – for I am up in the cold hairy mountains – a German Mercedes, colour white (same model as last year's ride to Damascus) winged its merciful way towards me along a vast stretch of open road. I leapt into the breeze and waved The Acts of the Apostles at it violently. There was the sound of a rushing mighty squeal and a hoot on the honker – it stopped dead. A miracle! All day I have been driving with two brothers who may be going to Teheran but they don't know. They are Iranian but live in Germany. Across the great plains of Anatolia we have sped, watching Kurdish farmers in the fields with their cart-loads of hay and fat bullocks trundling along the road.

The saddest sight I ever saw was a donkey standing in the middle of the road. He was shaking his head. All alone shaking his head, shake, shake, shake and stamping his foot into the ground.

He was a Potato.

Beside him lay a baby donkey quite dead, his head in a pool of blood. He had been hit and lay like a fallen soldier. The other donkey stood over him shaking his head, crying into the dust for he would not move for anybody – he would not. But the happiest story was of the afternoon when a crowd of Kurdish children shared a water melon with us. They were alive and gay.

I have every medicine under the sun except arse-itching cream! I have a disease of the arse-piece so bad that it is now even painful to sit down. If only I had a tube of "Antipeol". If only. I think I must have got jaundice or even cancer of the arse-piece. Here ends the news.'

Nine days out of Ostende when walking with pleasure along the road from Tabriz to Teheran the warm sun rose in front of me and the whole landscape made me feel as if I were walking without having to breathe. The Earth was glowing and the bare rocks were beginning to shimmer. How wonderful, I thought, to be abroad again – to be free. What car will I ride in next? Who will I meet?

'What lies beyond the hills?'

'FIRST THE LAND and THEN THE SEA.'

This was the answer to the question and in it there were the longings which I, Myself, longed for.

Now on that particular morning, in the silence of Persia, I was just saying it all to myself when I became slowly conscious of the grinding sound of a distant engine. Then I saw a thin streak of dust rising from the surface of the earth. I stood still watching.

Can you imagine me standing there with a pack-on-me-back and a Jordanian keffia wound around my head in the silence of Persia? Out of a dustbowl came a tiny speck of shining metal – it took an awful long time to become a reality . . . a reality . . . bump . . . bump . . . a Volkswagen stopped dead at my feet!

The driver, rather Oriental-looking, speaking fluent English of course, popped his head out of the window and said, beaming:

'Hello my friend, I'm going to Afghanistan, to Kabul, do you want a ride?' . . . And that's the magic of the road!

After three days at a speed that never exceeded 30 m.p.h. owing to the terrible ruts all the way across the Great Red Desert, we reached Meshed, a city not far from the Afghanistan border. It was there, at the most beautiful mosque I had ever seen, my friend Islam and I parted company; he to Afghanistan and I to a cheap hotel overlooking the bazaar which led in every direction to the Gawhar Shad Mosque.

Here is a letter written to Sir Keith and Lady Falkner after I had been locked up in my hotel by police for trying to take photographs of the forbidden sacred Mosque.

'. . . David Fanshawe is an animal who travels across continents and deserts. He is also a composer and photographer and a permanent pain at home. Don't worry he *will* survive but must nearly kill himself in the doing of the survival.

Islam, an Afghanistan economist, with whom I have been hitching for the past three days, has taught me many things about his faith and the more we talked and prayed together, the more we realized that our two faiths are similar. Washing ourselves in Persian streams like primitive apes, eating and sleeping on worn Persian carpets, drinking rusty water, we travelled over the earth's crust, thrust up or down or just plain flat.

Why should Christ have been the only Son of God? Why shouldn't God have had several Sons including Mohammed, Moses and Buddha? Anyway this journey has given me the seed of a new work. A work for chorus and orchestra combining Afghanistan soldiers' prayers with a glorification from the Christian Church. The prayer will first be heard sung by unaccompanied men's voices in Afghan ...'

A little later, in the same letter, I continued with a frantic outburst of fury and rage:

> 'Have I finished?
> I am so hot I must stop.
> I am so full of love and fight until I drop.
> God preserve us all and save us in trouble.
> God save our Gracious Queen and the caravan
>     routes from Samarkand to Constantinople.
> God stop it!
> The sun melts and all the ink drips.
> Stop it – STOP IT!
> I CAN'T, but I'm filled with love and visions.'

This letter was written in stifling heat, by the light of a small oil-fired lamp in Meshed.

In the eyes of the police, the manager of the hotel and everyone in Meshed I was an INFIDEL and an OUTCAST. All I wanted to do was to photograph the 'Sahn', the main bazaar which led into the sacred shrine of the Mosque, because it was so beautiful. Having failed, I had obviously been followed to the roof of my hotel and was seized at sunset, just at the precise moment when, by Oriental tradition, two magnificent trumpeters heralded the sun going down, a daily ritual in Meshed.

I fought the police, there was a scuffle and I struggled to 'snap' whatever I could of the Gawhar Shad Mosque but my camera was grabbed and police heaved me away by the arms.

'LET ME BE . . . LET ME BE . . . FOR WE ARE ALL ONE IN THE SIGHT OF GOD!' I bawled at the top of my voice.

It was midnight when I managed to escape from the hotel with my baggage and Sir Keith's letter. Climbing out of the window I jumped on to a flat roof below where a whole lot of bodies snored heavily. Clambering down a fire escape and reaching the street I beat a hasty retreat out of Meshed, on to the road which led me through wild, mountainous country to the farming lands of Gorgon, the Caspian Sea and over the Elburz Mountains back to Teheran.

At the house of Mr Massoumian, who had kindly given me a lift over the Elburz, I wrote an equally frustrated letter to The Parents:

'. . . I don't know what drives me, but I cannot find enough loneliness. I want to burn myself up with lovely torture in the hottest hole on Earth.

'I don't know what drives me but I am driven into the lonely places like a fly into a spider's web.

'Maybe the only way out is music? Maybe I shall stand alone one day in my own invention? Isolated in threads of sound – cut off from the confusion, the "is not possible" and "maybe" and "will ring you". One day I shall create my own desert which will join me to heaven and lift me out of my painful torture.' [Then as if trying to redeem the outcry with normality in the next sentence I wrote:] 'Spent a very jolly night last night with Dennis Fletcher and a crew from SABENA who flew in yesterday. Fletcher kindly took me out on the road to Isfahan and after a hard struggle in boiling sun I managed to pick up a lift. Apologies for this bad Apostolic – it's too hot!'

From Isfahan I hitched a ride in a truck full of goats and pissing cows up into the Zagros Mountains where I was hoping to find some nomadic tribes living high up in the valleys in their tents.

Higher and higher we climbed until, with relief, we were off-loaded at a mountain village. All fellow passengers got out, lined up beside the truck and said their prayers. After prayers I was introduced to a gentleman called Mr Parisi who was Headman of the Babadi Tribe. Mr Parisi was on his way to a certain valley in the 'high peaks' where apparently the Babadi had migrated from the oil fields near Ahwaz, which has been their custom for centuries. In the spring every year they leave the plains and migrate to the green pastures of the Koorang Valley. The only way of finding them is by mule. It was a journey which took us two days and at the end of it we were rewarded; there, in the most peaceful setting one could have imagined, we found the tents of the Babadi scattered like black stones on the hillsides, surrounded by golden corn and green pastures. Through the middle of the valley there flowed a beautiful, cool mountain stream.

Following the migratory paths of the Babadi alone on foot, I left Mr Parisi at a trading post after a few days, and trekked on across the Zagros until I finally reached a road and managed to pick up another truck which took me to the shores of the Persian Gulf. Coming down the mountains a wall of heat and humidity hit me which was so beautiful – exactly what I longed for '... to burn myself up with lovely torture in the hottest hole on Earth'.

Nothing could be hotter than the Persian Gulf in late August – sticky, intolerable and yet to me it was utterly necessary and everything I dreamed of.

## Bahrain – The Island of Pearls

Tom Fanshawe and Co. had been warned to expect me. They knew I was bound to turn up – but how, when, or from which direction was anybody's guess!

Having hitched all over Iran, I was eagerly anticipating a bit of fun on the island of Bahrain especially as Tom had two eligible daughters, Atty and Di whom I had never met.

Drawn like a magnet to Bahrain, my journey and subsequent

journeys to the Island of Pearls were to prove of enormous significance in my life – far more than 'a bit of fun!' From Bushire I hitched on a dhow, this time carrying camels and goats to Kuwait. The dhow 'Captain', who spoke no English, was told in Bushire that if he should meet another dhow heading for Bahrain, his English passenger would like to-get-on-it-mid-stream and would he mind making this possible in the name of Allah, the Infinite, the Compassionate, the Merciful.

Upon a green and steamy sea we set sail into a blackening sun. Looking down into the clear waters of the Gulf I swear I saw enormous sharks and horrible wriggling sea snakes. Then on the horizon, just as the Customs Officer at Bushire had predicted, we spotted one solitary, stationary ship. Urging the dhow Captain to approach, gesticulating wildly in case it might be going to Bahrain, I managed to persuade him, the dhow *and* the camels and goats to alter course until we were almost underneath the bows of an extraordinary looking boat called the *Kalachicken*. Hastily abandoning the dhow I clambered aboard up a rusty old ladder; but the whole thing was silent, everyone seemed to be asleep and the *Kalachicken* looked more like a modern version of the *Marie Céleste*.

When finally I found the *Kalachicken* Captain he didn't seem very sure where he was going and said that he had engine trouble and would probably head for Manamah (Bahrain) rather than Calcutta as he thought he would be more certain of getting the spares he needed in Manamah.

So waving the camels and goats goodbye, I took another hell-of-a-risk and became a crew member of what turned out to be nothing more than a 'factory ship' full of rotting shrimps, as the refrigerators had also gone wrong!

## Life On Board the *Kalachicken*

There were fourteen English crew, one Pole and a hundred and seventy-eight coolies from Bandar Abbas. The whole boat stank of rotting shrimps and it was even feared she was liable to sink. At regular intervals, the coolies lined up in rows upon the deck and prayed to Allah, the Infinite, the Merciful, whilst the Chief Engineer could be heard swearing loudly down in the bowels at the bottom as he waded about in a foot of oily sea water seething with rotting shrimps.

The following morning – still no progress, still no answers as to which direction we were actually taking. We were, however, still floating *on* the surface of the Persian Gulf, thanks to the prayers which Allah had answered.

Then another dhow approached from nowhere out of the steamy mist and with great excitement all the coolies leant over the side of the *Kalachicken* which immediately listed several degrees to port (or was it starboard?). The dhow came alongside, this time carrying large blocks of ice! The whole show was ludicrous and one simply couldn't explain in so many words *why* it took them all day to off-load the ice on to the *Kalachicken* while it quietly melted away in the boiling sun. In the late afternoon excitement rose to fever pitch and with One Horrendous Roar from the Engine Room, which sounded like a barrack-room Sergeant-Major swearing at his men back at Aldershot, the Chief Engineer cranked the engine and the whole boat began to shudder mightily.

Ali the Cook rushed out of the cookhouse and fell on his knees before the anchor chain which had begun to rise. Throwing his arms in the air he cried out with a loud voice in Arabic, which I don't suppose even the Infinite, the Merciful could have understood, as 'Chiefy', The First Mate, grabbed hold of him by his baggy underpants and flung him half-way across the deck exclaiming that the anchor chain was going to snap.

Then in the distance I heard a conversation which went exactly like this:

'AGI, FOOK!' (burble burble burble)
'FOOK!' (burble burble)
'FOOKING FOOK – AGI!' (burble burble burble)
'BASTARD!' (burble burble)
'FOOK YER' (burble) 'AGI!'

Agi was the unfortunate Cook's Mate with less brains than a snail and Sandy, Chief Engineer, suffered from ship's claustrophobia.

'Sandy fookin rownd bend,' complained Jimsky, the Pole on the Bridge.

'Sandy never git this crate to Barharain – 'ee gaws rownd and rownd in circles. 'Ave you seen Sandy's ankles yer fooker! What 'ee won't bundage fer on fookin ankles? Nothing rong with Sandy. But 'ee likes a Cool'en – 'ave yer git Cool'en fer Sandy? Then we might git some-where.'

A 'Cool'en' in *Kalachicken* language meant a Cold Beer, and poor old Sandy *had* been working in temperatures of up to 140°. He kept swearing that he was going to jump overboard but then Sandy swore a lot of things but never really carried them out. His favourite swear was about the 'Nixt flight 'ome on B.O.A.C.'

I wonder if he ever took it? Somehow I rather doubt it.

Our journey down the Persian Gulf was desperately slow as we could only achieve five knots, and at the end of three days, having helped Sandy out in the Engine Room myself, we finally managed to anchor in Manamah harbour, next door to the American Fleet.

With some embarrassment I got ashore in a Customs and Excise boat provided by the Royal Navy and having landed, walked up to Navy House – Headquarters of Commodore Fanshawe at H.M.S. *Jufair* – reeking of rotting shrimps, engine oil and nearly a week's worth of unwashed *Kalachicken* dirt.

'It's David, it's David!' shrieked Di, then aged about fifteen (pity!). Di's voice trailed away as she disappeared to get her mother, Joan Fanshawe, 'Uncle Tom Cobbly's wife', who seemed somewhat mes-merized to find me at that precise moment, swaying about in the sticky heat on the doorstep of Navy House with a desperately smart Flag Lieutenant, Richard Bush (Flags), who in all seriousness stood to attention behind me and saluted.

Unfortunately it happened on that particular day Joan was very busy entertaining Naval Officers' wives at a ladies' luncheon party, and hav-ing ushered me through the ever-open door of Navy House, I was invited to sit upon newspapers that had been put down on the dining-room floor as far away from the silver on the dining-room table as possible. I suppose it was just one of those unfortunate things, but for lunch the ladies were having prawn curry!

'HOW did you get here?' they kept asking. 'HOW did you say you got here? On a Rotting Shrimp Boat?' Their pretty little voices went up and down the scale like a set of untuned bells and from that moment on Commodore Tom's *outrageous* nephew became the focal point of all the cocktail gossip on the Island, and the ladies' afternoon was made.

## The Forbidden Beach at Hidd

Tom happened to be away on my arrival attending a course in England. In the meantime my desire was to explore as much of Bahrain and its neighbouring islands as possible and really get to know the local islanders. This was not altogether easy as certain areas had been forbidden to British personnel, notably the village of Hidd on Muharraq Island, across the causeway from Manamah, where the Pearl Divers lived.

Like Exhibitions, Moon Moths and Puppets, the Pearl Divers were to become another almighty obsession which started under cover of night when I hired a taxi from the centre of Manamah and told the driver, in my hopeless Arabic, to take me to Hidd and leave me behind on the beach. I then pointed to the boot of the taxi, opened it, climbed in and covered myself up in a tarpaulin because I knew we would have to go through a check-point *en route*. The taxi driver didn't seem at all surprised as he locked me up in the boot. We passed the check-point without any trouble and reached the beach where I spent an excruciating night under a dhow surrounded by the stinking remains of rotting sharks' heads – but I didn't go unnoticed.

At 'sparrow-fart' (5 a.m.) a Land-Rover with several British police drew up alongside my temporary residence and without any further ado smartly escorted me back to the Central Police Station in Manamah for questioning.

'What the bloody hell do you think you're doing?' shouted 'Ginger', a red-headed British police officer with a huge moustache.

'Didn't you know Hidd is prohibited? How dare you sleep on a beach in a restricted area – aren't you related to Commodore Fanshawe? Don't you think you might cause him some considerable embarrassment by your foolhardy actions? We've heard about you!'

With all the dignity that I could muster, which wasn't very much in the circumstances, I tried to explain why I was on the forbidden beach at Hidd.

'Excuse me sir, I'm sorry to have caused you alarm but all I wanted to do was to photograph the Pearl Divers and the boat builders of Hidd. In fact I found the area not at all unfriendly. Now would you please take me back to Hidd as the light is changing and I must get my photographs.'

'WHO THE BLOODY HELL DO YOU THINK YOU ARE – AND WHAT DO YOU THINK THIS IS, A RUDDY TAXI SERVICE?' he bawled.

How could this Purple One, who sat opposite me at The Table of Precarious Authority upon which there was a map of the Lands beyond the Sea, ever understand the need to go pearling, I thought, or the need to photograph the boat builders of Hidd, especially at dawn? The Ginger-Potato-He would never understand. All I could do was to try and persuade him that the world should have no barriers, no 'out of bounds', 'restricted areas' or 'prohibited beaches'.

'I'm simply a composer,' I said, 'from the Royal College of Music who has hitch-hiked from Dover across Europe, through Turkey and Iran down to Bushire and across the Arabian Gulf in a rotting shrimp boat. I've come to Bahrain to visit my Uncle for a holiday and I wish to write a Symphony and dedicate it to the Ruler of Bahrain and his people.'

Wearily the Purple-Potato-Pot-He rose from his seat, a little surprised I think, walked across to the window and stared at the Outside World for a long time before pronouncing *his* verdict. It was as if, for a moment, he had seen the light shining out of the Temple of Virtue because in somewhat quieter strains he said:

85

'Fanshawe, you're a bloody nuisance but a Land-Rover will take you to Hidd – you can take your blasted pictures provided you are out of there by midday. Do you understand?'

Fanshawe 'understood' but on that particular occasion never met the Pearl Divers and was soon reluctantly escorted back to Navy House bitterly disappointed.

Tom arrived from London knowing nothing about the Hidd adventure until he heard about it through the usual grapevine and at dinner one night commented:

'David, did you go to Hidd in the boot of a taxi and sleep on a beach under a dhow?'

'I did,' I replied, and proceeded to give Uncle Tom all the relevant facts and reasons why, because Tom likes facts and reasons why. Then Tom looked at me straight through his bushy eyebrows and in a loud voice, which must have thoroughly embarrassed poor old Joan who was sitting at the other end of the very long dining-room table, he announced:

'Damn good show old chap. I'd 'ave done exactly the same m'self at your age!'

The following morning I went down to the Naval swimming pool at Jufair and through the wire mesh fence which surrounded Jufair (for it was surrounded you know) I looked out across the balmy waters of the Gulf.

Out there, beyond the 'Out of Bounds' I could see the tiny figures of fishermen in little boats, white sails, and far away on the distant horizon the palm-fringed outline of Muharraq and Hidd. The sea was pale, quite flat and shallow and fishermen with donkeys were collecting their catch from the fish traps.

'Damn this wire mesh fence!' I cursed as I shook it violently and then proceeded to take at least thirty-six pictures of it on my camera.

You see, I found the wire mesh fence really rather beautiful and the pictures could be described as studies for they studied the blue of the Gulf and the wire mesh – in and out of focus.

How I longed to go in search of the Pearl Divers; but the rest of the community at the pool merely disregarded me. It was as if I were an embarrassment to them all, the Pearl Divers were of no importance to them and, after all, cocktail gossip *had* persuaded them that the Commodore's nephew was quite mad. However, the wire mesh fence and the freedom beyond meant so much to me that when I returned to Bahrain for the third time in 1970 – the journey on which I met Judith . . . must I go on? I managed to escape through a hole in the wire mesh and went to Hidd in a canoe – *we* got married (that's another story) and she drew it brilliantly.

*He went to Hidd in a canoe*

## Potato Meets the Ruler of Bahrain

I have great admiration and respect for His Highness Shaikh Isa bin Sulman Al Khalifah, the Ruler of Bahrain. We first met at the Ruler's beach which was one of those tropical paradises where Shaikh Isa had a seaside residence. Anyone who knows Bahrain, particularly those families who lived and served there, will remember His Highness's stately presence and frequent visits to the beach during which he often used to invite people to join him for tea. There, under the umbrellas, we would sit looking out over the sparkling waters of the Arabian Gulf towards Saudi Arabia. Tea usually consisted of lovely, gooey chocolate cake, the sort one finds at Fortnum and Mason, with a choice of either coffee or tea.

One afternoon I was sitting with Shaikh Isa and he happened to mention the songs of the Pearl Divers. At the time I had never recorded any folk music and it hadn't really struck me to do so before our conversation – besides I couldn't afford a tape-recorder. I found the Ruler most endearing and he even invited me back for tea the following Sunday, an invitation which I gratefully accepted.

Shaikh Isa welcomed me and allowed me to photograph him on the lawns of his residence which were being vigorously watered by a white-robed gardener. He then ushered me into his luxurious Palace which had brilliant coloured paintings all over the walls. We sat down on a beautiful sofa and a servant brought more coffee and chocolate cake. The room had an extraordinary collection of furniture and carpets and in the corner there was a wooden cabinet from which he quite un-expectedly produced a small red box which he gave me.

'This is for me, Your Highness?' I asked, as I couldn't think of any-thing else to say – hoping that it was for me.

'Please accept this small gift and remember me to your Uncle,' he said. 'Thank you for coming to Bahrain and I hope you will come back and see us in the future.'

Inside the red box there was a fantastic gold watch which I treasure to this day.

After tea the Ruler and I shook hands, we said farewell and I proceeded to hitch-hike back to Jufair. What a funny thing, I thought, here I am with a watch that's worth more than anything I possess and yet it's – back to 'the road'.

Potato!

Walking out of the Palace gardens, through the date plantations, another very significant sound penetrated my subconscious; a date picker shouted from the top of a palm tree 'HEE YOY YOY YOY YOY YOYEE'.

Then in the distance, through the filtering sunlight some women called back 'EBNY!' which meant 'son'. It was as if the world had become, yet again, a 'natural kind of Symphony' for another date picker cried out in answer 'HEE YOY YOY YOY YOY YOY YOY YOY'. He was followed by further cries of 'UMY!' which meant 'mother'.

I looked up into the palm trees and watched as date pickers lowered baskets of dates to women who were heavily veiled in deep mauve, black, purple and golden clothes. They took the baskets to a village made of dried palm leaves not very far away which I could just about pick out through the hundreds of palm trees. Once again my musical imagination was fired and as I stood waiting for a lift on the road, which had an oil pipe running alongside it, I began to imagine a Symphony for Voices with a date picker crying out 'HEE YOY YOY YOY YOY YOY!'

The end result was called *Salaams* and was not completed for another two years. It was first performed under the direction of John Lambert with myself singing both the part of the date picker and cantor with eleven other voices, piano and percussion at the Queen Elizabeth Hall, London, in May 1970.

*Salaams* not only marked my debut as Soloist but also as Composer on London's South Bank and to my complete surprise it received excellent reviews and became the first work in the Trilogy combining my Travels with my Music.

Here is an illustration, Exhibit Four, from the full score of *Salaams* which shows you what the cries look like on paper. Once again,

# African Sanctus

Members of the Jury who cannot read music please look at the exhibit as if it were a picture. Imagine the date plantations, the mystery of the desert and the Middle East. The whole musical effect is one of exuberance which resolves itself into ecstasies of praise in which the composer calls out to his friends in the Middle East, greeting them in the name of the One God.

*Exhibit Four – 'Salaams'*

## How a Camel Drank my Bathwater

*Another divertissement*

Down in the sands of the Empty Quarter on the borders of Saudi Arabia, having managed to hitch a lift in a light aircraft with a road builder to Abu Dhabi, I found myself in the hottest living hell I had ever known. There, I burnt myself up with 'lovely torture' – the problem was how to get out.

Now it happened, as all these things do, that I met a wild Bedu at an oasis who owned a terrible truck which he hoped to get back to Abu Dhabi; but the fiendish Bedu, not content with going round the sand dunes, insisted that he went up and down them instead like a ship tossing about in a thunderstorm. Not surprisingly he broke his axle and got himself severely stuck half-way up a giant dune.

He didn't seem at all worried ... he simply jumped down, lay underneath the damn thing and started to tie the two ends together with his turban. But it obviously wasn't going to work and I knew that if I didn't go off and get help neither of us would come out alive. At the time I remember having a high fever and dreadful diarrhoea.

SO.

Returning to the tracks in the desert which occasional supply trucks used, I began to walk in the direction of Abu Dhabi when to my utter astonishment I discovered an old Victorian Bath Tub sitting in the sand. Instead of taps the bath had a rubber pipe which soon disappeared under the sand – but it was enough of a pipe to hope for a miracle.

Stripping off all my clothes – shirt, shorts, unspeakable pants, rubber Dunlop shoes and the Jordanian keffia, I held the pipe up to the stars, as it was the middle of the night, and sucked, then shook it vehemently – then dangled it over the edge of the bath hoping that the 'Water Board' or whatever they had in the Empty Quarter would notice. THEY NOTICED!

Very slowly, even slower than the tap which fills our bath in East Sheen, drops of brown, rusty water began to trickle out. When the bath was an eighth full I proudly got into it, fully expecting it to be the last bath I would have before the Kingdom of Heaven . . . all of a sudden I swear I heard somebody creeping up behind me.

Shooting up, with no time to imagine what it was in case it might be a spear up the bum, I leapt out of the bath and found myself facing a camel. RESCUE! was the first word which came to mind once I had got over the shock. Perhaps Allah in his Infinite Mercy had sent me a camel to give me a lift back to Abu Dhabi; but unfortunately the camel and I were not on the same wave-length . . . nonchalantly a scraggy neck lowered itself into the bath and proceeded to drink all my precious bathwater down to the last, rusty drop. Then without a care in the world it sauntered off into the sand dunes and I never saw it again.

'BASTARD!' I yelled at the top of my voice running after it like a madman with everything flying in the wind; it was no good, the camel could run faster than I.

SO.

Returning to the bath I lay down and waited, quite exhausted, hoping that somebody would come along. It seemed like a lifetime of waiting. The sun, the most unwelcome sun, relentlessly rose out of a sea of sand and steadily got hotter and hotter as the whole desert changed colour from red to a blinding white. There was no point in walking so I lay under the bath and found what miserable shade I could. About seven hours later, having suffered enough 'lovely torture', I thought I heard an engine whining and groaning like a drunken oil tanker after a party the night before.

It was – and an even slower engine than the *Kalachicken's*, for it took a good hour to reach me. Across oceans of sand it approached at an angle of 30° to port, and its driver – the Bedu (crafty fellow) – finally came to a shattering and grinding halt at the foot of the bath. Triumphantly he leapt out and revealed the magic of his genius with a flourish. The axle was tied together not only with his turban but with nearly all the remnants of clothing and bedding he possessed!

Eighteen hours later we reached Abu Dhabi and the roughest ride I have ever had ended on a stretcher, for me at any rate. Unable to walk, suffering from terrible pains, I was carried to a waiting aircraft on a sandy strip of desert, flown back to Bahrain and admitted as a patient to the R.A.F. Hospital with an illness diagnosed as jaundice.

Apart from the generosity and kindness shown by Tom and Joan Fanshawe, not to mention the R.A.F. Hospital for having me, I had to admit I was extremely worried about my position with regard to my college career as the term had already started. Experience as an international hitch-hiker, however, had taught me that one should never hitch without one's life being insured. So having written an anxious letter to Sir Keith from 'the pit of yellow-guilt', my fears were completely calmed a few days later by his prompt and warm-hearted reply which I produce as evidence. Four weeks later I was passed fit enough to fly home – the fare paid for by the unfortunate insurance company. It was, after all, the best 'hitch' I ever had – a direct flight from Bahrain to London on that old V.C.10!

*Exhibit Five*

Telegrams: "Initiative, Westphone, London"
Telephones: "Kensington 3645 (3 Lines)"

**ROYAL COLLEGE OF MUSIC.**

Prince Consort Road,
South Kensington,
London, S.W.7.

KF/UT
FROM THE DIRECTOR.

21st September, 1967.

David Fanshawe, Esq.,
R.A.F. Hospital,
Muharraq Island,
Bahrain,

Dear David,

We are all extremely sorry to hear of your predicament. Mr. Lambert has just shown me your letter written on Monday last the 18th. If you have jaundice it will be no use me telling you not to worry. I know only too well from experience that you will think this is the end of everything. You must now do what the Doctors tell you and have a complete rest, forget all your projects and get better, I am sure you need not worry about anything here about your further study. Arrangements will be made to postpone things until you are really better.

This is a very hasty note. I have five minutes before the post. We shall hope to have good news of you soon. Meanwhile take it easy and count your blessings. You have a lot. I was delighted to have your letters en route during the past weeks which I found extremely interesting.

All good wishes,

Yours sincerely,

*Keith Falkner*

Keith Falkner

## *A Mighty Upheaval to Find Oneself*

Imagine any composer of which I am just one.
No composer really knows his destiny.
How is one able to create something out of
  nothing?
One was once created oneself,
But then so much creativity seems to fall on stony
  ground.
I WILL NOT BE WASTED – I WILL NOT!

Imagine a Great Somebody and ask yourself
  'How did He or She do it?
  Why did They choose the path They trod?
  What clay was moulded by which Potter,
  That They might have been Bach or any
    Superstar of your calling?'
For we are living Now and we are part of Time.
WORDS ARE NO GOOD – WHAT WE WANT IS
ACTION.

### *fff*      'ACTION!'

That is why I tell everybody about myself;
To strengthen myself;
To do something and not waste other people's
  time.
Creative result, however humble, is after all only
  an offering to the Potter whose hands shaped
  one's beauty –
And, I agree, there are some who are more
  beautiful than others!

It is The Audience who matter.
THEY are the Dreamers and I would like to give
  them
SOMETHING TO DREAM ABOUT.

*Comment:* It's easier looking back in the light of experience, but at the time, on those early journeys, I couldn't quite visualize how to combine travelling with composing. After all, there were no father figures I could emulate and it wasn't a question of going to study Electronics with Stockhausen in Cologne, or of writing string quartets, concertos and other types of avant-garde ditties.

Sometimes I wish it was.

As I've already mentioned, the development of this Epistle is like a symphonic build-up in waves of cacophonic experience towards the dilemma which ultimately faced me when I set off on my journey up the Nile from Cairo to Lake Victoria, during which time I produced a mass of evidence written in the form of letters to the Ralph Vaughan Williams Trust. Out of it came *African Sanctus*; but in order for you to experience that journey to its fullest, whilst reading the letters and their accompanying commentary, I still feel it important that you should be further drawn into the dichotomy of my existence (a somewhat painful one) which was to lead me yet again into the paths of Adventure and Exploration.

Next time with a resolute ambition – TO RECORD THEM.

# V

# Journey to Iraq and the Arabian Gulf, 1968

It was another long, hot and exhausting journey from Dover docks to Baghdad. My objective this time was to visit the 'Fertile Crescent', go down the Euphrates in a canoe, across the southern marshes of the Hor al Hammar where the Marsh Arabs live and return to Bahrain from Kuwait.

For the first time I carried with me a rather inferior cassette tape-recorder and hoped to record unusual sounds as I went, particularly the songs of the Pearl Divers. As yet my journeys were not sponsored and I had to make do with what little funds I had, notably a £33 holiday scholarship from the College.

The journey from Dover to Baghdad took ten days, hitching as usual – surely a record? On arrival, armed with a letter of introduction from the British Council, I looked up the telephone number of my only contact, a Mr Geoffrey Hancock, who was then First Secretary at the British Embassy, and hoped I would at least be rescued, given a bath and a jolly good meal. Perhaps it was too much to ask, to drag an overworked diplomat to the front door of the Iraqi Petroleum Company, where I ended up, and expect him to wet-nurse *another* hitch-hiker whom he had never actually met. Little did he know that he would be appearing in my memoirs six years later!

Having got over the initial shock and finding that I was house-trained, Geoffrey and his charming wife Amelia welcomed me in and from that moment on we have been the best of friends and never lost touch. In fact during the composition of *African Sanctus* Geoffrey, then posted to rural Shepperton, England (poor old Geoffrey), made many helpful suggestions, notably that I had forgotten to include the Crucifixus in the Mass.

'A Mass without the Crucifixus can hardly be called a Mass', he said.

Geoffrey is not only a diplomat, but was once an Organ Scholar at University, and I know he would agree with me when I plead with you, Members of the Jury, that it is no good reading this Epistle without hearing my music.

In Baghdad Geoffrey and Amelia introduced me to many kind and wonderful Iraqi friends who gave me my first real understanding of folk music – I therefore have a great deal to thank them for. One of those friends was Basil Ali Hateem from Mosul who is mentioned at the climax of *Salaams* when I greet all my friends.

Having hitched up to Mosul on the River Tigris I then returned to Baghdad and went down to the South of Iraq to Kut where I became the only European guest of Shaikh Hilal Bilasim Al Yasin. At that time his family were mourning the death of his brother, who was very much respected in Iraq.

It was an extraordinary experience – for many days I sat with Shaikh Hilal's family, brothers, relatives and distinguished visitors who had come from all over the country. During the day we listened to the Imams reciting the Quran in the Palace gardens overlooking the Diyala river, and at night more than two thousand women could be heard in the harem, beating their breasts and wailing the loss of their beloved leader. Early every morning tribesmen would come racing into the Palace grounds on horseback, firing rifles into the air, performing war dances which they called 'Hosa!' A typical gesture of faith and comradeship.

The mourning period went on for forty days and was known as *el-Arbi'iniyeh*. Out in the desert the Tribes rallied and camped in long, communal tents, feasting on mutton and rice, drinking endless cups of very strong coffee served from lovely copper pots.

As principal guest I had the honour of eating alone in the Palace whilst other visitors watched from behind. It was a bit embarrassing as I found myself daily confronted with two whole sheep, two five-foot mountains of rice, Chinese chickens in bowls of jelly – which all had to be eaten at the rate of knots. Without washing one's hands one was then expected to indulge in a delicious pudding which could best be described as a kind of blancmange which one shook in one's right hand, having used the same hand for the previous course. As you must already know you never use your left hand when eating food in Arabia. The left hand is only meant for 'other business', Members of the Jury.

It was during this period of mourning that I began to think a great deal about the possibilities of combining the sounds and adventures of my journeys with my compositions.

## Into the Marshes of the Southern Euphrates

*Strophic tanboura sympatico e scordatura (abnormal tuning) e molto saltando*
The musical indications above, faithfully noted from *A Student's Dictionary of Music* by William Lovelock, D.Mus., have been reproduced here so that you can imagine exactly the type of music you would expect to hear in the marshes south of Babylon, known as the Hor Al Hammar. Very contented, the Marsh Arabs play their one-stringed fiddles (Rebbaba) as they sit 'at home' in the evening on mud islands under the watery sky, having come in their canoes from the Central Lakes with giant reeds for building huts – much as in the days of the Old Testament.

Playing the Rebbaba with a small, curved bow they manage to create a nasal quality which the buffaloes enjoy very much.

*Saltando* in the Hor Al Hammar, means that you place the bow upon the string, usually made out of thin wisps of reeds, and you 'scratch' at it with the middle of the bow. You accompany your 'bowing' with your voice as you sing about the day's work, the heat, the height of the reeds you've seen, or how many trading dhows you watched going to Basra – once upon a time, during the Great Flood when Noah took all the animals into the Ark . . .

At night I slept in reed huts with the Marsh Arabs and in the morning the whole world looked as if it were nothing but a Sea of Reeds. In between the reeds one travelled by canoe through narrow water channels from one reed village to the next.

Whilst canoeing across the marshes I wrote another sort of poetry-letter to The Parents, but having no knowledge whatsoever of the names of Iraqi plants and what-not, I refer to two kinds of Lily which intrigued me very much as I drifted towards the Shatt Al Arab. I call them 'Nana-Weed' and 'Crod' and they represent a Lily and a Weed respectively. Just imagine them for a moment and you will know what I mean!

'. . . It is flat and it is strange and in it there are the reeds. Ever since I have been Him standing on a "Chic Weed" gazing out to sea, I have longed to be in a place far away.

In a native canoe with a man in a towel and pole I have deepened into the marshes from the River Euphrates and have seen the Buffa-Blows sniffing in the air by the place where the Nana-Weed grows with the Crod.

The Crod he is all smelly and stiff and the WOT HOG greeds on the Nana green weed who floats and gurgles with the Frogolites.

SNAKS skirmish the yellow brown skum and the puff of the Buffa-Blows heats the reeds from a gurgling hole in the swim.

A little wooden boat with a shirt and a kettle and placement full of reeds, all hanging, drips along and the stench and Nana-Weed come along also under the burning sun.

*He* looks for a Mosquowtoe but he finds none because it is too hot and because 'ee Crod says,

"He Mosquowtoe must go until floods come in the months."

Lying down in the evenoon-bath in the bottom of the boat with a hand dripping out to catch "The Bill", he floats with his being on a ponder where the World stops moving and becomes what-he-longs to be.

A beautiful sight under the sky.

High-things and ginger whiskers startle in the breeze above the weed and the sprinkle of a Kingflash wing, flashes, swoops and burps!

In a flourish the whistle wings dart and dash in the sky.

On a little mud clot the village is made of reed mats, and little flies buzz in a million.

In a dream the sails drift by and the man stands like a white ghost against the purple sky – his stick is a ten-foot rod which prods at the Nana-Weed as he glides by.

It is flat and there is only reed and sky and reflections in a pool as wide as the earth is high.

It is where HE is happy to meet his longing and wishing-well, where the Nana-Weed grows with the Crod and the WOT HOG pokes and Kingflashes whistle forward to catch what he can while the Crod-'ee sits and giggles with delight.

The world passes by.'

## The Pearl Divers of Bahrain

*With urgency in the present tense to be read very quickly and never mind the English*

For the second time I arrive on the Island of Pearls.

It is September 1968 and I approach once again through the haze of the blackening sun on a dhow from Kuwait. Ahead I can see the palm-fringed beaches and the masts of the dhows in the Old Harbour of Manamah.

This time I come from the Euphrates in the way that the traders used to come in the days of Ur and Babylon. I am in search of the Pearl Divers, writing in the present tense because they are always present – in my heart, in my mind and in my imagination.

I arrive and start asking questions.

On this occasion I discover that only four ships are out pearling. Where are all the others? Fifty years ago there would have been One Thousand Ships – but now only four.

No one will take me to the pearl beds, so I go to B.A.P.C.O., the Oil Company, who say they will assist. A launch party is arranged and a helicopter goes out to the pearl beds where the Divers were last seen, but that was yesterday. The pilot returns saying that he cannot find them anywhere – 'They've vanished', he says.

B.A.P.C.O. don't give up, the launch party is ON!

Twelve hours later we return, exhausted, after an endless search up and down The Gulf – NO PEARL DIVERS.

Most of the Divers are now dead. Only a few, like Ah'lan, the great blind Pearl Diver, are living – he knows all the songs of the sea.

I meet Khalifa Shaheen, son of a Pearl Diver, who now makes films for B.A.P.C.O., he is a cameraman and says he can help. He arranges for a bus to be ready at a certain time on Muharraq Island, the other side of the Causeway.

Why? I simply don't understand.

Khalifa and I get on very well – we meet and start a journey, the strangest journey I've ever been on – to collect the last remaining Pearl Divers and to take them to an isolated beach on the far side of Hidd where they will re-enact their songs and chants of the sea.

As the bus belts off I cannot believe my ears. Sixty Pearl Divers start chanting . . . Oh My God, Listen!

Mingled with the sound of the hooter of the bus, a deep chesty roar bellows forth as the Divers begin to sing. Khalifa explains that it doesn't matter where they are or what they travel in – for them the motion is the same.

In going, they are reminded of the Sea.

We arrive at the beach far away from the town – out there on the edge of the shallow waters by the fish traps. All the Divers get out . . . And then . . . An extraordinary ritual.

They tie an old rope to the wheel of the bus and pretend it's the anchor on the end of a chain. They sit on the sand and begin the drama of Pearling on Land.

They are no longer needed at Sea.

They sing a sequence of never-ending songs – beginning with the act of pulling on the rope, which Khalifa explains is the longing they have in their hearts as they return to the Pearl Beds. Then, they begin to row the boat.

The roar of the Divers becomes ONE RHYTHM, united they bellow as their leader, old Ah'lan, wails to Allah asking for his merciful protection upon their journey. Instead of oars there is only sand.

The Divers drop anchor and then – and then – large circular tambourine drums are heated over a fire so their pitch will ring out over the Ocean, over the Sand. The Divers, each one dressed in a brilliant white garment, begin to dance upon the deck – upon the sand.

If you listen to *Salaams* you can hear them in the distance – the quality's not good enough so I'll have to return.

I am here with the Divers on Sand; I'm here with the Divers. A jet screams overhead as it comes in to land at Bahrain International Airport. It's the Old with the New.

Now the Divers pretend that it's dawn, the oysters are opened as they sing one of the songs each Diver has known since he first set out to sea.

This is 'The Song of The Dawn'.

In my *Symphony of the Arabian Gulf* you will hear it – a magnificent, moving, powerful and magically beautiful song.

The Divers are sitting in a circle on the dhow in the sand. How long can this last? Will Ah'lan be alive when I return?

This is the story I tell John Inglis Hall, the author and poet, when I arrive back in England. I tell him everything – all my experiences, all that I feel, all that I see.

In 1968 he responds with a poem which must become a text for the second work in the Trilogy of Travel and Music.

*Symphony of the Arabian Gulf*

> White sails, white sails, white sails.
> Centuries of sails,
> white under the fierce blue sky,
> mirrored, and moving
> down the winding river
> to the far blue sea . . .

## Journey to Iraq and the Arabian Gulf, 1968

O blessed stream of time,
now bearing me!

For God be praised,
I too have seen those sails,
white like the gliding gulls,
filled by the old warm winds
that blew those antique hulls.

Who would be a modern traveller?
His seat in the sky
is a chair in a winged box
with a glass eye.
His earth is a map
through a gap
in the white wool clouds . . .

That is why

I chose a timeworn ship,
broken and deep-sea rusted,
fish-scented, shell-encrusted,
to cross that emerald sea.
At night, I savoured the smells,
heard the sea and the engine-room bells,
and an Arab song pitched high.
Till the day that a dawn came up
when I woke and the red sun rose
on the curved horizon's line.
There lay the pearl of islands,
the island of pearls . . .

Bahrain!

Bahrain, Bahrain, Bahrain.
Once, your blue sea had wings,
white sails, white sails, white sails.
And divers risking life
to deck the crowns of kings.

To search for the last
of the winged fleet
that pearled in the green deep
where seaweeds sway like dancers
and the pale sand gleams,
I took ship from the old port.
They were rare, rare as phantoms . . .
Only the great tankers,
majestic above the lost pearl-beds,
musical with their sad sirens,
were not things of dreams . . .

Bahrain . . .
Like the shell of an oyster
with a pearl at its heart,
born of a grain of sand,
ancient, awaiting a finder . . .
As pearls lay deep in your sea,
a darker treasure
lay deep in your land.

Bahrain . . .
Like the shell of an oyster.
Ring of the emerald sea.
Ring of the sands and ports,
haunted by men long vanished,
but now by me.
Ring of the new city,
shade, shade of palms,
with rattling fronds.

## Journey to Iraq and the Arabian Gulf, 1968

Women, black-veiled,
feet whispering in the dust.
Heat and the water-sellers.
Song of the frogs at dusk
in their limpid ponds.
Ring of the crumbling mosques,
the arched tombs,
palaces, lonely, desolate . . .

Then, at your very centre,
under blown sand
and the eternal thirst
of rainless soil,
Rim Rock of the desert
and the new black pearl –
Oil!

Bahrain, Bahrain, Bahrain!
White sails, white sails, white sails!
One with the new treasure . . .

The dhows drift, fishing,
in the fading light.
The red sun drops
into the milk-blue sea
of evening.
A gull takes flight.
The Muezzin calls and chants.
A sailing tanker sounds,
solemn and deep and serious
above abandoned pearls . . .

*John Inglis Hall*

## Second Journey Home from Bahrain

This time returning from The Foreign I wrote to The Parents filled with a new awakening.

'Dear to the First of all,

I want to tell you some things, but I suppose you will wonder what it's all about, and then you will think your thinks and come to a conclusion of importance like me.

ME is the importance, and THEE are the owners of ME so THEE are all "importuanté" immediately also.

I have almost come to the end of my long and HOT.

It has been a successful one and I have thunk-alot.

I have collected fifteen hours of original music and have analysed much of it with experts in the art of it.

I have done four broadcasts, two television shows and some newspaper interviews.

I have slugged my passage through and through complete into the Marshes, into the Deserts, into the Mountains and into the Lands of Milk and Honey muchly.

I have dripped upon a stone.

I have roared like a thunder noise and have spoken politely everywhere also.

I have scandalized, shocked and caused gossip.

But I have been understood better than before.

My life is full of PRAISE and my language is music.

I have seen the Pearl Divers and watched them singing and dancing. Some of them fell down and cried with huge rags to wipe their faces from the tears and sweat. Their way of life is finished, they are a finished crew who stand upon a sandy deck steeped in ancient customs and traditions.

I sing with them, bash their drums, dance with excitement like a madman in the street.

Cause a traffic jam, with all the children in Manamah beating drums.

Imagine the "Pied Piper of Bahrain".

"Who is this dreadful Exhibitionist who rolls around the streets . . . ?"
Cocktail gossip I overheard.

MUSIC is my LANGUAGE.

FILM is my PICTURE.

TAPE is my SOUND.

I want to play, play, play the music of one country to the music of
another half-way across the World.

The more we listen to each other's music the more we shall understand about each other's background and culture.

ONE SOUND must shimmer like a mirage . . . ready . . . waiting.

ONE SOUND waiting to be uncovered, like a piece of jade, ready to
make its listener unbelievably happy.

I am nothing but I shall continue to serve God through Music and I
shall fill my egg life with sail, enough to blow me round the Orient and
back to praise him who blew the wind straight to carry me there.

I have made a plan completely and now I ask God for the guts to
carry it out at all cost.

It is with tremendous expectancy that I shall arrive at Dover docks
upon a morning.

Expect me, therefore, on Thursday the 3rd on the crest of the
English Chanhole and I will be exceeding to see the people muchly.

I am as usual.'

## African Sanctus – Initiations

Before the 'Ceremony of The Letters', the Witch Doctors have
advised me to give you a simple cure which will make the reading of
The Letters less painful and more enjoyable. The cure is quite a lovely
one and involves a bit of magic in the form of a prescribed medicine
which people have been using for centuries.

The Letters are, therefore, to be published with further illustrations
and exhibits according to the Ordinary of the Mass and it is further
advised that Members of the Jury listen to the recording of *African
Sanctus.*

For the Spirit of the Witch Doctors has now entered into the heart of the Patient (the Defendant) who has responded, like Masai Warriors who purge themselves before venturing upon a long and dangerous journey.

*African Sanctus* could be the Ultimate Cure, if the Eyes of Eternity agree that it is – but from now on the Doctors say that any further evidence in this Trial must be gathered together according to the stages of the 'Sanctus Journey' into another Secret and headed:

KYRIE

GLORIA

CREDO

INTERLUDES

ET IN SPIRITUM SANCTUM*

CRUCIFIXUS

AFRICAN SANCTUS

THE LORD'S PRAYER

AGNUS DEI

GLORIA

CODA and ULTIMATE CURE

The original Letters can be found at R.V.W. Headquarters and are contained in a particular volume. At the time they were written with no intention that anybody other than the head Witch Doctors of the R.V.W. Trust – namely, the Committee, Mrs Ursula Vaughan Williams, Miss Williams and possibly the spirit of R.V.W. himself should read them. But the Hippo Man, Elders and Witch Doctors have now informed Bwana Collins, the Publishers, that before the Patient can be ultimately cured of his diseases and complaints he must stand Trial because the Court says that it cannot do any more curing unless the Patient be found 'Innocent in the Eyes of Eternity'.

The Sanctus Letters and their accompanying commentary are,

* A slight irregularity in the Order of the Mass owing to dramatic events which affected the Defendant's journey through the South of Sudan.

therefore, of vital importance and three other points must also be taken into consideration:

Firstly, with part of the sponsored money the Defendant at last bought himself some respectable equipment.

Secondly, The Letters were addressed to a certain Miss Williams, secretary of the R.V.W. Trust and no relation to the composer, whom the Defendant had not met. During the Sanctus Journey she became for him the embodiment of someone who cared. When he returned he was disappointed to find that Miss Williams was not only married but had a son aged twenty-one.

Thirdly, before departing up the Nile, the Patient had had an unhappy love affair with a Swedish girl which had ended tearfully at Waterloo Station. The after effects left him lonely within himself and longing for some love.

### *A Tribute to the Witch Doctors before the Sanctus Letters*

> Why all this space?
> Only thirty years or so?
> If only I were longer
> I might have seen more.
>
> But the Doctor says
> 'You're lucky!'
> The other Doctors say
> 'Sanctus, Sanctus, Sanctus,
> Dominus Deus Sabaoth.'

Rattling their stones and Secrets they repeat:

> 'Sanctus, Sanctus, Sanctus,
> Dominus Deus Sabaoth.
> Go and learn something
> Oh my Friend,
> Mr David –
> Go and learn something.
> HURRY!'

# VI

# *Kyrie*

'. . . Dear Committee and anyone else who might be interested.

I have had a good day.

First of all my bottom has dried up and secondly I have at last recorded in the Mosque. How was it done? Well, I shall try to explain although I never was much good at our language.

In general it must be understood that in Egypt I am having to fight two wars – one political and the other religious.

I carry around with me in a black hold-all case some very alarming-looking equipment and have no letter of permission to be doing so. I am naturally suspected everywhere I go and have now been in police stations exactly four times answering up. Each time it gets worse and twice my hotel room has been broken into.

To continue.

Today, Friday (Holy Day), I decided that this was it – so with the invaluable help of an Egyptian Coptic Christian (a very brave man) we set off in a taxi for the old city at noon – object, to record the Muezzin (Call to Prayer) from the market-place and to make an attempt at getting into the Mosque under cover of a confusion to be set up by my Coptic Christian friend.

Further object, that the recording of the Muezzin be harmonized one day with a choir singing the Kyrie of the Mass – the Arabic becoming a brother to the Greek. In other words –

"Allahu Akber, Allahu Akber, Kyrie eleison, Kyrie eleison."

S O.

Lying low in the back of the taxi I managed to poke my concealed microphones somewhere in the general direction of the hubbub from the market place as we drew up alongside the entrance to the Mosque.

Then suddenly up she went – wild and woolly right across the market square:

"AL ... LA ... HU ..."

The Muezzin had begun.

In hundreds the people hurried to the Mosque leaving market stalls in the care of women and children.

Jumping out of the taxi, leaving rubber Dunlop shoes behind, I leapt into the crowd with the tape recorder still recording (stereo $7\frac{1}{2}$ i.p.s.) closely followed by my brave Coptic Christian Friend. As I entered the Mosque (copying all the others) I raised my head above the crowd – coughed and burbled:

"ALHAMDU LILLAH" meaning "THANKS BE TO GOD".

No one seemed to stop me and before I knew it I was already kneeling down in a vast, long row of "fellow Muslims" following their every move. The black hold-all was beside me and the microphones, now erected on a small portable stand, stood firmly on a thick red carpet under the brilliant glittering lights hanging above.

My shirt, far too large, also red, partly covered up the microphones – I remained breathless, crouched in the holiest position I could find and prayed very hard hoping that R.V.W. would hear me!

The seconds ticked by and the prayers of the Faithful filled the whole building. It was wonderful. In rows we stood – bowed – knelt – stood – bowed – squatted and kissed the red carpet. The Quran was recited and the Imam chanted his magnificent order as a deep hollow chorus of voices answered:

*ff* "AH ... MEEEN ..."

So full was the Mosque that all the little back streets had the Service relayed through loudspeakers – most people prayed on reed mats.

Eventually I got out as I came in – borrowing someone's apron without him realizing it. In retrograde:

"ALHAMDU LILLAH" – cough – and dash for taxi.

Coptic Friend anxiously waiting – scarper – the two of us in taxi – we escaped out of Cairo up the hill to the Citadel – SCARPER – relief – the tape was still recording as I hadn't dared touch it in case we were caught – once on the open road, making sure no one was following, I opened up the black hold-all – stuffed microphones inside – then –

HORROR! (*sffz*)
NOTHING! (*agitato con poco furioso*)
SH – (*very bad word*)
NOTHING!

Not one damn thing recorded since that flute player outside the British Embassy.

EXPLANATION (simple one): In my haste to switch on the record button in the market place, I must have pressed the pause button at the same time by mistake whilst taking my shoes off.

MACHINES! (did R.V.W. like them?)

Finally, with the help of the Coptic Christian's security card, we *both* managed to enter the Citadel, a beautiful Mosque built for Mohammed Ali the Great. Here the Service had ended. Here I achieved my first major success in peace and quiet.

Together we persuaded an Imam from the Mosque to give us a special performance of the Muezzin inside the great dome of the interior.

In almost complete silence his mellow voice echoed all around the building. Somewhere, in the soft light, two microphones quietly recorded the sound which has hallowed so many battle-ridden walls for so many centuries.

For those who have not heard a Muezzin, particularly an Egyptian one, and for those who may never find themselves in such a peaceful place overlooking the distant glimmer of Cairo on the eve of what may turn out to be yet another war, I hope to bring this magnificent sound to their ears.

If I can achieve my aim and if someone would care to listen without

Jordan, Wadi Ram – the beauty of dawn in the desert

Valley of the Shadow of Death – a tiny Greek monastery

prejudice, then perhaps the two worlds – Christian and Muslim – can be joined together one day on a concert platform.

I send my best wishes and hopes for another day.

Yours sincerely Fried Eggs.

(nom de plume de ma tante) . . .'

Now in order for someone to write to the R.V.W. Trust and sign himself 'Fried Eggs', that someone must have been pretty alarmed – but I really felt it necessary, having been questioned so many times by the police, as I feared all my letters were being intercepted.

It was a time of great anxiety for the Egyptians and of course, they suspected every move I made; any ambition of recording 'the folklore' was out of the question. No one would give me a research permit and recordings had to be made discreetly. I was never badly treated and quite understood why the authorities were so concerned – I was motivated simply by a passionate desire to hear the people of Egypt singing and dancing.

One morning at the British Embassy I met a school-teacher who invited me to visit his home in the Delta, another prohibited area. Abdul Latif Moty had just returned from studying in London and was very keen for me to meet his family in the market town of Zagazig. He seemed sure he could arrange for the farm workers in the area to perform folk music and gave me several letters of introduction to help me get to Zagazig. In his innocence and in mine, neither of us realized just how difficult it would turn out to be.

'. . . so I set off yesterday with a friendly farm labourer in a crowded train from Cairo Station with two letters of introduction from Abdul Moty. Tying a handkerchief round my head I sat in the train and placed my friend's baggage and some bean shoots from the market on my lap. All was marvellous except – if caught – NO PERMISSION.

I have learnt very well to disguise myself – I rub brown boot polish into my face. Result – two farm hands travelling to Zagazig!

The bluff worked and on arrival I reported to the station master's office. Abdul Moty soon arrived and expressed his great joy very loudly

Bahrain – the date picker who called HEE YOY YOY YOY YOY YOY.

at my arrival, but he was also confused because I didn't have "the Permission"!

He said it would be easy to get this from the Ministry of Interior in Cairo, but I'm afraid I know a little better.

The bluff ended at the police station and do you know it took them exactly seven and a half hours to decide that I could spend One Night with Abdul and his family and that in the morning I must return to Cairo to get "the Permission".

We left the police station in a horse-drawn carriage under a full moon around midnight and arrived at Abdul Moty's house. His wife was expecting us – peeping round the corner.

First of all I was offered "The Pyjamas" (an Egyptian custom), lovely ones – thick – with no hole in the front – very good for relaxing.

Then I was offered a shower and a very late supper specially prepared – rice, chicken, eggs, cheese, bean soup and honey, after which I was invited to sleep on a large double bed *with* Abdul Moty. He seemed to prefer sleeping with me rather than with his wife, but in fact he was only being a real Egyptian gentleman, giving me protection in his home because I was his guest.

Early in the morning Abdul's two little daughters looked at me shyly. All together we played a queer kind of hand-shaking game, after which I was shown where to shave, where to dress, where to sit and with much reluctance how to leave with a guide in a horse-drawn carriage for the station, with a promise from Abdul that I would be returning "tonight" if I showed a certain letter which he had written, to a certain high official in the Ministry of Interior who "without question" would sign his name for "the Permission".

I somehow fear I shall never return to Zagazig. Already it feels far away; but I'm very glad I went there as I managed to get a lovely view of the Delta from the train. The area is quite beautiful and to actually see the countryside again is such a joy. The train rushed past fields of cotton and in the bright, flashing sunlight, figures could be seen stooping and bending as some lazily journeyed along shadowy glades between the fields, returning on donkey or camel, whilst others leaning low, washed themselves in the numerous canals – some just slept under the bushes. If only I could just sleep under a bush and wander about in the fields. These people, the "fellaheen", are the people of Egypt – these are the people I am longing to be with. They are the ones who can sing and dance.

Can the police sing and dance?

NOTHING! THEIR BOOTS ARE TOO HEAVY!

I send my best wishes,

Fried Eggs . . .'

I shall never forget the frustrations of being cooped up in Cairo unable to record the music of Egypt. Those weeks, however, were not spent in vain, due mainly to the encouragement I received from the Institute of Folklore and with the particular help of Emile Azer Wahba who assisted me in recording a Coptic Christian Mass, several Muezzin calls and sound effects from the Mohammed Ali Mosque and the 'Friday' celebrations from the Ataba Mosque.

I was also given permission by the Director of the El Azhar Mosque to go every day and study the techniques of reciting the Quran and the 'Call to Prayer' and it was there, in the Azhar Mosque, I learnt how to sing the 'Call to Prayer' myself.

The Muezzin which accompanies the Kyrie in *African Sanctus* was one of the recordings I made in the Mohammed Ali Mosque. An Imam kindly sang it several times, specially for the recording, and the interior of the Mosque in which he sang leant its own unique resonance to the overall sound, with distant taxi-hooters from Cairo City adding a ghost-like quality in the background.

In 1972 I wrote the Kyrie for unaccompanied choir and Muezzin. The technique used is not unlike one which most composition students practise; namely that of harmonizing a Bach choral in four parts and adding a fifth part, a 'cantus firmus'. In this case the recording is the 'cantus'. Here is an extract from the full score, Exhibit Six, with a literal translation of the Muezzin and Kyrie. Together they represent a prayer of unity between the Muslim and Christian faiths.

*Exhibit Six – Kyrie: Call to Prayer*

God is Great
God is Great.
Lord, have mercy on us.
I witness there is only One God,
Lord, have mercy on us.

I witness there is only One God.
Lord, have mercy on us.
Mohammed is His Prophet,
Christ, have mercy on us.
Mohammed is His Prophet,
Christ, have mercy on us.

# Kyrie

Come hurry to prayer,
Lord, have mercy on us.
Come hurry to prayer.
Christ, have mercy on us.
Come hurry to do that which is most needful,
Lord, have mercy on us.
Come hurry to do that which is most needful,
Christ, have mercy on us.
God is Great
God is Great.
There is only One true God.
Lord, have mercy on us.

# VII

# *Gloria*

*Luxor – et lux perpetua*

> Go and learn something
> Oh my Friend,
> Mr David –
> Go and learn something.
> HURRY!

The only way one could possibly learn anything in Egypt in 1969 was
to take the train south from Cairo to Luxor and become a tourist.

'. . . does it matter if it's Rome, Cairo, Luxor, Athens, Madrid or
Tangiers? The spiel comes out the same and the guide book soon looks
lost after the ticket barrier.

I prefer to know nothing and remember nothing rather than a whole
lot of "tonic-dominants" – who was buried where and with what gods
and at which dynastic period etc. – does it really matter?

Undoubtedly they *were* buried but how the burial was achieved is as
great a mystery to me as all the wisdom in the Fertile Valley.

They were dead and buried and they ascended into heaven, of that I
am sure, and they sat upon the thrones of their gods and brought with
them their souls and magic but they left behind their earthly goods.
You can see these quite easily with the guide in the museum!

There are the mountains (Theban Hills) and they stretch in a chain
all along the Nile Valley. In 1922 Howard Carter and Lord Carnarvon
set about discovering the Valley of the Kings. What they have achieved
is something so fantastic my mind is absolutely-completely-boggled,
but then I am a very bad tourist!

In fact I greatly admire the other sort of tourist because he has so much brains and money with masses of film to spare and I do really believe he understands his guide and goes home to his home-movie regurgitating word for word the spiel he has been told. If one *must* follow a guide for God's sake do it in the open air where there isn't any echo.

With the aid of a muleteer I set about discovering the tombs for myself from the top of the Theban Hills.

Avoiding all risk of tourists and guide books we camped in a small village to the west of the mountains and at dawn began to climb up a rugged pathway. Like an eagle I sat upon my mule and looked down into the wadi below. My mule did not slip.

I was about to go down into the earth from the sky as the sun rose over the Nile Valley. There was no sound except rocks.

It was a dangerous journey so I just clung on at an angle to the stirrup.

It was as if I were being swallowed up into the tomb – not just one tomb, but some forty open mouths – black – and looking at me like air-raid shelters.

His name was TUTANKHAMUN, RAMESSES I, RAMESSES II, AMENOPHIS IV, AMENHOTEP, SETY I, MERENPTAN – and his Queen was a woman who bore him as many as a hundred and one sons and sixty-seven daughters (I may have got it wrong) but, HE didn't land on the Moon – HE didn't reach Berlin or photograph Mars.

He surrounded himself instead with all his knowledge and his Spirits and keepers of Holy Oil; his boats passing through the under-world – his enemy the serpent.

He decorated the walls of his tomb with all these things and he buried himself surrounded by his treasure and his God-shaped head was protected by his "Mummy". He was King of Egypt – He was a Ruler beside a River and he called himself PHARAOH.

*Et lux perpetua* – do you know the bit I mean in the Requiem by the French composer Fauré?

"ET ... LUX ... PER ... PET ... UA".
Have you got the sound in your head?

Let eternal light shine on them.

At this point I stood at the tomb of TUTANKHAMUN and that bit went round and round in my head – the harmony divided from the tune and I was left – looking – hardly able to believe the "middle parts".

*Et lux perpetua* – all the way through the mountains to the River Nile. Let eternal light shine on them as it does today.

The river is alive with activity and the donkey driver makes money from the tourist – and rightly so!

My guide led me through fields of sugar cane – past little villages of mud where man and woman meet in the earth and mate with their bodies in private.

Their burial ground is the wet, alluvial soil of the river and their waterpot is still of clay.

> What a beautiful sight to stand by the banks of the
> Nile and watch.
> When a woman comes she carries her water pot so,
> When she goes it goes like this.
> I find this strangely erotic.
> It fascinates me.
> But then I suppose –
> So do we all.
> *Et lux perpetua* – AMEN . . .'

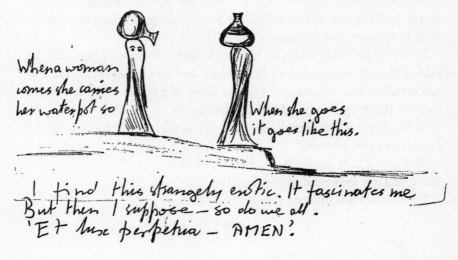

When a woman comes she carries her waterpot so

When she goes it goes like this.

I find this strangely erotic. It fascinates me
But then I suppose – so do we all.
'Et lux perpetua – AMEN'.

One night I took a sailing boat from Luxor with a guide. It was a very still evening as we ventured up the Nile, so still that we were becalmed.

Away from all restrictions, prohibited areas and in relative safety I began to record the magical sounds of the Nile lapping up against the boat. In the distance, quite by chance, wedding celebrations gradually became clearer in the night. Hypnotic rhythms got louder and louder as we crossed over the river and beached the boat near a village. Rushing on ahead through a banana plantation I approached in a great hurry – my heart was pounding and I hoped the villagers would be friendly.

So often one hears music just like that – without any warning; one can only hope to be received and greeted as a friend. On this particular occasion I was lucky. Everybody in the village had gathered in the moonlight as a wedding-band played to guests who were seated in rows in a circle around them. Pushing my way through the crowds I leapt on to a rostrum where the band was playing and holding out my stereo microphones on improvised booms (bamboo poles) I managed to produce a recording of maximum vitality which is heard at the opening of the Gloria in *African Sanctus*.

Here is the translation fusing Islamic secular music with the Gloria and a prayer which expressed the total feeling of wonder I experienced on the Nile.

*Egyptian Wedding Song: Gloria and Prayer*

When she comes with her beautiful veil,
  Glory be to God in the highest
When she comes with her beautiful make-up,
  And on earth, peace to men
When she appears with a face like the moon,
  Of good will.
And skin like cream,
  We praise Thee;
There she expects to find her Bridegroom,
  We bless Thee;

Waiting –
  We adore Thee;
God blesses them with plenty of sons,
  We glorify Thee.
And prosperity.
  We give thanks to Thee
God will keep them happy and increase love,
  for Thy great glory.
Passionately between them –
  O Lord God, heavenly King,
Praise be to God who unites man into woman,
  God the Father almighty.
Praise be to God who makes Two into One;
  O Lord
Praise be to God who makes Two into One
  the only begotten Son, Jesus Christ.
And Two into Many.
  O Lord God, lamb of God,
  Son of the Father.
  Thou who takest away the sins of the
  world, have mercy on us.
  Thou who takest away the sins of the
  world, receive our prayer.
  Thou who sittest at the right hand of
   the Father,
  Have mercy on us.
  For Thou only art Holy;
  Thou only art the Lord.
  Thou only, Jesus Christ, art most
   high.
  With the Holy Ghost
  in the glory of God the Father.
  Amen.

# Gloria

Let us pray.

All pray silently with the priest for a while.
Then the priest says the opening prayer to which
    the people respond:
Each person in his own way;
In his own right;
With respect,
Honour,
Faith.

## By boat through Nubia – October 1969

'. . . I'm sitting on the upper deck of the s.s. *Ibsis*, a fascinating paddle steamer some fifty years old belonging to the Sudan Navigation Company. I write by moonlight with the aid of a flickering lamp. Lying on narrow wooden floorboards on either side of me, surrounded by the curious smell of chocolate cake oozing up from the cookhouse, are the stretched bodies of camel drivers from the Oasis of El Obeid, to the west of Khartoum. They sleep remarkably silently and the whole deck is littered with their white clothing – some of it flaps slightly in the breeze.

I am leaning on a stand resting up against a clay water pot from which we drink neat Nile water – I wish it had a little gin in it!

It's one of those rare moments in life when one is part of the past. In fact the s.s. *Ibsis* is three boats strung together with rope – the 'puffing billy' part in the middle has a rotating paddle at the back. Here and there, there are green plants for our entertainment and I suppose we make about two knots as we glide gracefully over the top of the world – over the floodwaters of the Nile to Wadi Halfa.

We've been sailing now for two days and a short while ago we accidentally crashed into the top of a sand dune with a heavy thud, for we are floating over the desert in the time of the flood, if you know

123

what I mean. I was flung out of my bunk and have just been told we are to rest here until dawn when we shall make the last few "knots" to Wadi Halfa.

Besides the bodies on the deck we have an equally curious selection of nine Europeans. There are two German doctors, going to study flowers in Ethiopia – two French ethnologists, man and newly-wed wife from Lille, going to record the history of Nilotic civilization on an island called Sai – one English model, married to a naturalized Hungarian-Canadian who is emigrating to South Africa in a Volkswagen called "Love Bug" with his small son (whom I rescued today from a rather large cooking pot); he belongs to his former mistress, an opera singer from Düsseldorf. We have another Frenchman who speaks no English and ME (Musician).

I am now sitting on a wooden casket containing some very scraggy – sad – dozing chickens.

Too uncomfortable!

The camel drivers have been on the move for four months and they now return to El Obeid by steamer and third class railway carriage having sold their animals in Upper Egypt.

I have been forbidden to record any music on ship as it is the "High Dam" but I have just got away with the strains of a plaintive melody about a "girl who leaves home and is loved by her mother as much as by her lover!" The singer, a camel driver, I caught down on the lower deck by the "Love Bug", he happened to be singing.

The rocks are very black against the brilliant moon.

Since I was a boy, gazing out to sea standing on a "Chic Weed" at West Wittering, I have dreamt of Africa. When I went back (to school) I always went – to AFRICA.

The journey has taken me twenty-seven years.

Black Africa looms over the horizon – tomorrow it's Wadi Halfa then the long trek down the White Nile to Dongola (Kitchener's Dongola before he relieved Khartoum).

There's a man standing – gaping at me in the moonlight – he is motionless. What IS he thinking?

I long for the belly of Africa, I long for the stampede in the Elephant Grass – the native dances – the throb of hearts burnt by the sons of Blue Mountains.

I long to bring back their music and express my feelings with the recordings.

No Englishman will ever click his fingers like an African.

Tomorrow I travel south, God permitting me a safe return. The English may have left Sudan, but as soon as one arrives one is aware of the discipline, smartness, correctness and a certain charming, casual manner with which the customs officials deal with you (could almost be Dover docks!).

"The Dock" is a flat-bottomed punt sitting half in flood water and half on sand. Beyond – half a dozen Land-Rovers are ready to strike out across the desert.

We have arrived – SUDAN.

Across the floodwaters of the "High Dam" one can see the tops of buildings, including a Christian Church, just sitting in the dazzling, shallow waters of the flood. Every year it gets a little higher.

I listen for the solemn note of the church bell in the shimmering waters but all I feel is heat. This is "Old Wadi Halfa engloutie". New Wadi Halfa is a few wooden huts resting along the end of the railway line surrounded by miles and miles of desert.

Like a madman I set off immediately across the sands for I love the desert passionately and having been cooped up in Egypt I can now let fly.

I lie in the sand and cover myself in it and then go up into the rocks for shade and prayer. At sunset I return to the water's edge to bathe and bask in the dripping sun.

No one can know my joy at such freedom and my love of the waste land. I need no one – I just need nothing – rather this than *all* the old ruins put together!

Now at last security seems lax but just for precaution I am posing as a French archaeologist going to Abri – for as luck would have it my French friends from the boat are going there tomorrow.

In case I get stuck I have recorded a vital message on my machine in Arabic which will satisfy the Chiefs of all the villages down the Nile. The message was recorded by a school teacher in Wadi Halfa who says:

"David Fanshaouwee is an Englishman coming from the Queen of England – Her Majesty Queen Elizabeth the Second sends messages of goodwill. He wishes to record the music of your village for his country and would be grateful if you could provide him with musical entertainment which Her Majesty will greatly enjoy in her Palace. Please help my friend Mr David and greetings." '

### The Island of Sai – Nile, Sudan

Having become in the eyes of the Sudanese authorities a French archaeologist, I hitched a ride in the roughest and toughest truck you have ever seen – made in Japan. It took eighteen hours to reach Abri and the Island of Sai where I became a guest at the archaeologists' remote mission station. I described my impressions to the R.V.W. Trust:

'. . . imagine for a moment a high desert plateau fringed with a thin strip of cultivated land, palm trees and numerous mud brick villages. Rising high above the plateau (the Island of Sai) you can see isolated mountains, sand dunes and heat haze. If you climb to the top of the island you will look down on a vast stretch of fast flowing muddy water – the Nile. It's amazing how vast it is.

For the first time since I left Cairo I feel at last cut off. There is no road – no electricity – no television, radio, telegraph service – no noise except nature – no engines on the Nile – not even the sound of a gas cooking ring.

Travel on the island is by foot, camel or donkey and I have finally reached a place where no one suspects me.

There is a strange, green-coloured lizard looking at my left foot.

My research begins as it usually does – with a "recce". So I set off across the island to discover what sort of people they are, whether they will play me their music, how they live and whether they are friendly or unfriendly.

I crossed the desert to the top of the plateau and walked down to the cultivated strip where I suddenly found myself in what appeared to be a completely deserted village of white, baked mud (depends upon the angle of the sun), in the burning heat of the afternoon. On principle I carry no cameras, recorders or baggage.

You can be sure that *you* see no one but everybody sees you. The black windows are full of eyes. The dust makes a dead shuffle underfoot and one is followed everywhere by a miniature sand storm kicked up from one's feet.

I feel like a cowboy in Texas!

If only someone would come out and shake hands and walk with me, one would not be so exposed. Then it all began; I met Mohommed Abdul Ali Mohommed – a boy of about sixteen who immediately impressed me with his "Exercise Book". I read some sentences he had written in English.

"ALI HAS A DONKEY."

"MUSICA!" I said and began to dance in the dust. It is lucky I am by nature an exhibitionist – it doesn't do in England, but out here such a demonstration helps to break the ice, for sooner than I had expected, from several dark doorways, I was joined by children – each one with their exercise books.

"Jibli moya" (bring me water) I said.

That was it!

"The Headmaster" came out, greeted me and invited me into his house and since that moment he has been my constant guide and interpreter.

For three days now I have been living in the village and last night everybody celebrated – MUSICA!

First the little boys, then little girls, then the older boys danced to the accompaniment of an "Oud" (mandolin). The music was Nubian in character and not unlike music from Upper Egypt. It seems as though the people living on the Nile above the third Cataract are settled land-owners – not very accustomed to travel for they live in almost complete isolation and I believe this is why their music is very tuneful – has a simple rhythm but lacks the power and tremendous rhythmical drive of the music of the seaboard areas – Red Sea, Indian Ocean, Persian Gulf etc. Their voices are clear – not throaty, their chests are thin, beautiful, warm and not expanded by centuries of hard labour. They do not "rasp" like boatmen for they have very little to do with boats – this I find quite a revelation since they live on the banks of the Nile.

The school seems to be the centre of village activity apart from a tiny mosque. There operates here a simple system of education, rather like our boarding school idea. As the little boys come from all over the island they live in the school for two weeks at a time and then go home for a weekend – this is due more to the fact that there is no transport on Sai.

Discipline is most impressive and I think the heat naturally tends to make one speak slowly and quietly. In class there is complete silence. The Headmaster has absolute control and I get the impression that every boy is glad and happy to be in school – every boy is proud.

Yesterday I was invited to teach all the boys a lesson. I am not a teacher – but I felt that I was expected to *be* a teacher and that a lesson was very important.

So, this was the lesson and it lasted fifteen minutes. With the aid of a few simple hand signals we spoke – I also wrote on the blackboard.

| ME | BOYS |
|---|---|
| YOU | (pointing) |
| | YOU |
| ME | |
| | ME |
| HE | |
| | HE |
| LOVE | |
| | LOVE |
| PEACE | |
| | PEACE |
| NO WAR | |
| | NO WAR |

# Gloria

I LOVE YOU

                              I LOVE YOU
I LOVE PEACE

                              I LOVE PEACE
I LOVE PEACE NO WAR

                              I LOVE PEACE NO WAR

The lesson ended with the following words which were spoken:
"Alhamdu Lillah" meaning "Thanks be to God". The boys replied,
rbled, then laughed!

It is very hard to understand that what in fact looks primitive
(absolutely prehistoric) is not what it appears.

How a man lives with his wife on Sai is as sophisticated as my Aunt
who lives with my Uncle in Hartley Wintney, Hants.

One has to be so careful to judge what is – not what *you* think should
be.

I have never seen such clean people – cooking – sleeping – eating –
LIVING. They have a whole code of existence just as my Uncle has
when he catches the 8.10 from Winchfield Station.

I thought, when I arrived on Sai, that I was amongst uneducated
people – I am sorry for my "think" because I now know better.

The World is a strange place – if a man lives like he does why not
observe – love him – then depart. If he already believes in God why
should he believe in your God? I would not want to change this island
for all the Electric Cookers in the World.

When the sun rises – it is light.

When the sun sets – it is dark.

Twice I have stumbled across the island in the pitch black and have
not seen one light anywhere. At night the whole world is dark – no
moon – just the other worlds twinkling far away . . .'

In those days I was desperately searching for 'tribal music' but without
experience in this field it was like looking for a needle in a haystack. I
thought I was searching for the real thing, but then what is the real
thing? Was the music I found on Sai tribal?

Africa was beginning to emerge as a far larger and more complex continent than I had ever imagined. I realized it was going to take me years of research, not just a fleeting glimpse here and there. When I listen to those Sai recordings today I hear in them something very different – something modern which can be heard regularly on Radio Khartoum. In fact all I had achieved was a few recordings of religious and secular music influenced by modern communication – notably the transistor radio. Other music from that region I would describe as 'work songs' – camel drivers praising their animals, water well songs praising the fertility of the soil and the odd disembodied strains of melodies coming from scattered plantations.

With a preconceived notion of what tribal music *ought* to be I naturally felt disappointed (rightly or wrongly). At least I was learning.

In my heart I wanted to discover the music of Africa, and lured on by the visions of early explorers I proceeded south, hitching in many trucks. One night at the town of Shendi I suddenly heard a tremendous commotion. Leaping up from where I was sleeping (under a truck) I set off in great haste in the general direction of the 'source of sound'.

'. . . In Shendi I heard strange drum beatings and wild shouting – following the noise I pushed through the crowds on the outskirts of town.

Began to record but was beaten up severely by hundreds of people with donkey sticks and thrown out into the dirt.

Students dragged me to a lovely garden somewhere and apologized most profusely saying that the Gallaheen people thought I was making a film and that they did not understand I was only recording – Fanshawe never gives up!

I returned badly shaken and very bruised but continued to record standing on a wooden bed behind seven sweaty drummers with a great black, fat woman who dripped rhythm everywhere and recited the past glories of the warriors of the Gallaheen. This was the ritual dance of "Penis Cutting" (circumcision), most erotic and exciting.

# *Gloria*

After the students had explained what I had come to do I was very soon accepted by the people and continued to dance myself, thrusting a donkey stick high above my head, squatting down in front of the great black lady – I shook like a native and loved it until I was drenched in sweat and dust.

The following day across endless desert I rode for twenty hours until finally I heaved my baggage into the B.O.A.C. office in Khartoum where I had a contact, Peter Johnson, but I'm afraid he just looked at me with an expression of utter bewilderment.

There are times you know when one can do nothing about it – I regret I deposited a little pool of dust in his office.

Am now preparing to go to the far west of Sudan to a mountain which they say is like "Paradise" where strange people live.

Must dash, putting this on B.O.A.C. flight tonight – so this is just a reminder for those of you who *can* fly that you would probably be far happier and Better-On-A-Camel!

Here ends the news . . .'

# VIII

# *Credo*

*Journey through the Marra Mountains – West Sudan*

'. . . have just received a kind letter from Miss Williams persuading me to write more! I need no persuasion for I would give my life if necessary in order to achieve my objective which is to bring back over the next few years, whilst I have bones to fight with and a heart like a tiger, the music and excitement of people with whom I am deeply in love.

You cannot imagine my joy when I discover music that is played and sung by people whose Rhythm – Attack – Breath Control and Space baffles me.

When the women dance with their outstretched fingers across their chests – when the men woo them with noises like old steam engines puffing up the line – when I slip into their gentle trances after my work is done and recite with them the Muezzin and the old familiar words of Mohammed. Perhaps I am just a bad Christian?

GOD is what matters and there is plenty of him out here . . .'

I am now inside myself shouting out to everyone what it is that matters to me most. If I comment, it is only to re-live those dynamic moments which I shared in the Marra Mountains with a tribe known as the Fur.

I BELIEVE IN SOMETHING –

I'm travelling with a spirit inside me which is leading me up into the high places, into the paths of unknown territory, unexplored heights of musical greatness. I am writing – I am writing – to The Parents, to the Spirits of my Ancestors, to Anybody who might listen for I believe in one God, the Father almighty, Maker of heaven and earth; and of all things visible and invisible.

'. . . now living in a village of native huts, African style, trying to discover what sort of music the Fur tribe make. My hut is situated in a field of maize on a gentle slope which goes down to a fast-flowing mountain stream.

In such a place it is best just to listen to the birds and bees humming in the trees. The wind rustles the corn and the women, half naked, go down to the stream. They look like stone-age ladies – much more stone-like than the men who could easily be imagined getting off the tube at Oxford Circus . . .'

> Go on,
> Oh my Friend,
> Mr David –
> HURRY!

'. . . I am going – up into a village called Kalu Kitting a few days' camel ride from here. I am looking for a man who plays the "Moorlay", a kind of flute, whose name is Shirtie Abduli Busrah.

All day until sunset we travel, the three of us, my two Fur guides with camels. The chin of the leader is like rough sandpaper and I have just led him away to a quiet place under a knotted tree. Together we sit in the dark and he sings me a song about his camel:

For I am a brave man and I travel alone with my camel.
I am not afraid even at midnight.
My camel comes from the Nile where there is much water and
    grazing.
Because of this the ancestors of my camel are of the stronger type.
My camel is strong because it belongs to that race.
My camel shortens the journey better than any other camel.
My camel is Busharrin [named after a tribe who live on the Nile],
It is white in colour.
My camel shortens the journey by day and in the night time,
    my camel leaves me with no fear.

What is it about the Fur? They make one feel like a King. It's the way in which the women approach the men, not only when they dance but when they meet each other along the way. If a man is approaching a woman it is the duty of the woman to bow very low and greet him with pleasure and respect. Methods of greeting are after all, indigenous to us all – "How do you do?" From place to place the meaning is the same but the way in which the greeting is said is so varied. In the Marra Mountains the opening to any conversation always starts like this:

The woman says to the man "Afaili konga (Good morning) to which he replies "Afaili konga" (Good morning). She says "Afaia" (In good health?) and he replies "Thiabin" (Goodness reigns). She kneels and waits . . . he approaches, usually on camel.

She says "Afaia" and he replies "Thiabin". Greetings then continue – in musical terms one might say *molto accelerando* (getting quicker and quicker):

"Afaia?"
"Thiabin"
"Afaia?"
"Thiabin"
"Afaia?"
"Thiabin"
"Afaia?"
"Thiabin"
"Afaia thiabin?"
"Afaia"
"Mmmm Mmmm" (she hums)

The woman then gives out a warm resonating hum from the depths of her soul it seems, at which point I am almost falling off my camel completely seduced!

"Mmmm Mmmm" (she hums again warmly)

The conversation then develops and the business of the day is finally discussed. That there is still time in the world for such things gives me a new breath for doing things – like a second wind.

Each village in the Marra contains a "Shirtie" or Ruler who has under him a number of "Omda"; they are like counsellors.

If a woman has a problem she comes to the Shirtie's home where he is usually sitting with his Omda in a circle on straw mats. She kneels right down outside the enclosure of the home. There is usually a kneeling post behind which she kneels.

usically 'a behind thich When the "Shirtie" speaks hugging hush her

kneeling post she kneels.

she answers, the ground to request politely.

When the Shirtie speaks she answers, begging the ground to hush her request politely. The answer comes quite quickly and then she raises herself – keeping her back upright – she leaves and takes a piece of my heart with her as she goes.

Yesterday I saw a woman feeding her child under a thorn bush tree. Her breasts flowed with milk and she looked *so* beautiful as she rested on her journey in whatever shade she could find. Wiping herself she rocked slightly – a large yellow butterfly drifted by and the camel men brought her water. She had a special way of wrapping herself up in her blue cloth, tying the bundle of child to her back – its little head sticking out – it *looked* at me but I don't think it saw me, only another part of the world which it just accepted.

For a long time we rode in a little procession. No one offered the woman a camel or a rest from the carrying of her "something" on her head. She insisted that she walked behind us and when I showed her the way before me she smiled, shook her hand and walked instead behind me.

Now an Englishman sitting on a camel is a ridiculous sight! POMPOSITY at its worst.

One thinks one is so wonderful sometimes, especially on a camel – like Lawrence and things, but the fact remains one is a complete amateur and as bad as a Grade Four cellist trying to play the Fauré Elegy. Incidentally if anyone is interested in the magic of Fauré I do wish they could hear Madame Nadia Boulanger talking about his music. She is surely one of the world's greatest musical souls – when I am in her presence it is like my bafflement and admiration for Fur dances; like a great tennis player – all around the ball is space.

The fact is these camel men are about half my size and when they sit on the animal they become part of it! When I try I am simply an ugly obtrusian.

Obtrusian = Obstruction in my language.

Besides, my bottom is too soft and after four days of perilous mountaineering on the thing I prefer to walk. This is part of the old Bedu custom – at dawn you walk for three hours until the sun is well up. Sometimes the end of the camel quivered over the edge as it tried to get a hold. Rocks dropped away beneath me. At other times I was simply landed in the middle of a thorn tree! You can see the damn thorns coming at you as the camel pushes on regardless – you shout and grab the branch with wild fingers to stop it – you duck – "oowhoowh" and other unspeakable words you shout as it tears at your hair. You see the point is *you* are riding slightly higher than the camel and the trees being "bush" are slightly lower. Do you see what I mean?

It was after such a day – I think the third day – that I was in despair. I said to myself on my camel, "What the bloody hell *am* I doing?"

It was one of those fine days which one looks back on with a tremendous sense of pride at having done it and even the thorns and tummy aches and (arse) itch and so on become a pleasure to remember.

It was in fact, I should say, the most important day of this whole journey because, almost like a reward, I was just getting into my sleeping sheet beside the fire under a "Bird Song Tree" when I heard something far away which made me sit up and shout "Vaughan Williams!" That is my shout for action – that means – down tools – up – unpack tape-recorder – microphones – tape – check batteries – fix microphone leads, adjust headphones and collect spare batteries (I have this operation down to 1 minute 10 seconds). In haste I hastened off into the brilliant moonlight beyond.

My heart beat and thumped and again I heard fantastic singing like some modern composer only *much* better – it got nearer – I climbed up a steep bush-covered hill and entered the compound of a village. Climbing over stone walls and knocking a barking dog for six with my foot plus a stone, I jumped into a hole beside a hut and peeped over the top. Already the recorder was running.

Like the Omda, four men in a trance sat on a mat swaying from side to side, and the most extraordinary singing came out of them. I crept forward and, unnoticed, placed my microphones on a small tripod right in the middle of them.

To describe such music is an impossibility but I realized there and then that perhaps this was it – the link between Arab and African music – the link I was searching for.

There I was, out of breath, panting, trying to be quiet, fearing that someone might spear me, fearing that I might be caught in the act, having to think all the time about "quality, good stereo" – and then to my horror, having come all that way, I found my batteries were flat! Dashing down the mountain, that bloody dog got in the way again and I tripped and fell over a rock. I've never run faster in my life, all the way down to the bottom. I reached the camels under the Bird Song Tree and groped in the dark for spare batteries. With pockets bulging, I began the arduous climb again to the top, hoping that the incredible singing would continue.

I needn't have worried. The four men on the prayer mat carried on all night and never even knew I'd been there. Their chanting consisted mainly of a dissonance of a major second to a semitone resonating in a "four part Canon" in which each voice carried two types of entry. One of "Attack" and one of "Entry". The text was religious, taken from the Quran (recited from memory) but it seemed to have strong African influences in rhythm. One could say that the Canons were made up of *modulating rhythms*, like many hairy composers who submit equally hairy works for competitions and who invariably run off with all the prizes!

After such a find as this I went off into the hills and exploded upon the mountain in a Soliloquy which lasted until day-break. For God be

praised I received extraordinary strength that night and realized exactly
how the chanting of the "Four Men on the Prayer Mat" could be
combined with Western choir and percussion. I fell down before the
moon and wept.

The place was called Kora . . .'

### *Quran: Gospel: Camel Song and Creed*

In the Name of God, the Merciful, the Compassionate
Praise belongs to God, the Lord of all Being,
the All-merciful, the All-compassionate,
    the Master of the Day of Doom.

Thee only we serve; to Thee alone we pray for succour.
    Guide us in the straight path,
the path of those whom Thou hast blessed,
not of those against whom Thou art Wrathful,
    nor of those who are astray.

      I believe in something –

Deo gratias.
    Thanks be to God.
Dominus vobiscum.
    The Lord be with you.
Et cum spiritu tuo.
    And also with you.
Gloria tibi, Domine.
    Glory to you, Lord.
Verbum Domini,
    This is the gospel of the Lord.
Laus tibi, Christe.
    Praise to you, Lord Jesus Christ.

For I am a brave man and I travel alone with my camel.
    I am not afraid even at midnight.

I believe in one God the Father Almighty,

# Credo

Maker of heaven and earth,
And of all things visible and invisible:
   And in one Lord Jesus Christ,
the only-begotten Son of God,
   Begotten of his Father before all worlds.

Born of the Father before time began.

My camel comes from the Nile where there is much water and grazing.
Because of this the ancestors of my camel are of the stronger type.
My camel shortens the journey by day and in the night time,
   my camel leaves me with no fear.

God of God, Light of Light,
   Very God of very God,
Begotten, not made,
   Being of one substance with the Father,
The Father, The Father!
   Patri, Patri!
By whom all things were made;
   Who for us men, and for our salvation,
Came down from heaven.

Qui propter nos homines,
   et propter nostram salutem descendit de caelis . . .

If only this page could become the sound of my music,
   Then you would hear it,
An intoxicating rhythm.

The Credo and the Four Men on the Prayer Mat
   are part of the Ultimate Cure which is beginning to work.

The Patient has composed the two sounds together,
   The Patient has already begun to Glorify his Creator.
The Patient is being cured.
   Hear it!
HEAR IT! For it is the Blood of Praise.

# IX

# *Interludes*

When I woke in the early morning having finally fallen asleep under the Bird Song Tree, my guides were already loaded, having collected a few other people who wanted to join us on our wild and dangerous journey across the Marra to Kalu Kitting. Slowly the little procession started off, winding its way through the stony pathways as you can read in a letter written to The Parents:

'. . . Camel riding is just like Grandpa sawing logs – it is obstinate. But please give Grandpa my special love and think and tell him that without his obstinacy I would not!

There is a lot of Grandpa out here – also tea drinking is like Uncle John eating cornflakes at breakfast!

I am now very excited about my travel – it is working out and more than anything I never lose sight of my ultimate goal and objective.

As I go along the way I repeat a little saying over and over again, gritting my teeth as I do so for it is very tiring and exhausting work –

"God's work *will* be done – God's work *will* be done – God's work *will* be done – I WILL – I WILL – I WILL – God's work *will* be done etc. etc."

I send huge emphasis and explosion upon my shoulders from above and love and sadness too on my pilgrimage – because in the end I am bound to fail to achieve all that *should* be done – it is too much.'

This kind of fanaticism didn't go unnoticed by Them at Home and I know there were times when The Parents used to get very worried about my mental condition. Travelling into the unknown is no easy task and one is inclined to become very isolated, withdrawn and utterly resolved in one's determination to achieve an objective. This is the great thing about lonely places and lonely thinking. One blows oneself up out of all proportion and yet in that proportion there lies strength. By the time we reached Kalu Kitting on the way to Zalingei my hands had a terrible skin irritation caused by the heat, the rough journey and in particular the rope which attached me to my camel. A camel is no easy animal to steer across the mountains. This skin irritation I refer to in my letters to the R.V.W. Trust.

'. . . On arrival at Kalu Kitting I was very tired and the trouble with my hands had worsened. I wrapped them in a sheet because all the skin on my fingers was tearing off in shreds – in search of food I stumbled upon a wonderful man called Saleh Adam Gasim from Zalingei who spoke fluent English and who had been working on a project for the United Nations making a survey of the water supply in the Marra Mountains.

Now Saleh told me there were to be "Celebrations" the following day at Zalingei, so abandoning all hope of finding the Moorlay player, Shirtie Abduli Busrah, we roasted a chicken, drank two bottles of Steem (locally brewed wine) and walked, or should I say stumbled, for ten hours through the night to Kass. Saleh carried my heavy pack and after a lovely meat stew in a funny old road-house – I hesitate, because there are no roads – we heard the distant hum of an engine.

"TRUCK!" I shouted.

Sitting high up on the top, my legs dangling over the edge with about a hundred white-wrapped black and brown faces crowded in behind me on boxes of oranges from Nyala, I proceeded towards Zalingei. The night air was bitterly cold and the trouble with my hands meant I had to tie myself to the boxes on the truck as I had no feeling in my fingers.

On arrival Saleh decided first of all that I needed a wife, so he took me through a maze of very neat straw huts until we came to a clearing amongst tall trees. The brilliant moon and the distant sound of dogs barking excited me and made the prospects more alluring.

Three girls were called – suddenly all the feelings in my fingers came back and for the benefit of all you Benevolent Musicians at home I do recommend to you a wife from Zalingei!

For the sake of the record only, their skin is like velvet . . .'

The celebrations at Zalingei were luckily postponed for two days. This gave me a chance to recover with my wives. (Unfortunately I'm now reduced to one wife!)

On the appointed day excitement increased throughout the market town. Literally thousands of people assembled on the Football Pitch and at about 4 o'clock in the afternoon the Celebrations began. On such occasions it is customary for tribes to gather in groups, each one with its own special type of dance – each one competing against the other for the most attention.

'. . . their dances are enchanting to watch, one in particular where the women line up in a circle opposite the men. They enter the circle and choose a man by pointing at him, the man then in ecstasy lets off a high pitched yelp of delight and leaps into the ring which eventually forms itself into two lines of women opposite men who dance in a trance. The dance is accompanied by beautiful female singers dressed in long, colourful clothes who are answered by a chorus of men and rhythmical hand clapping . . .'

# Interludes

## Zalingei Celebrations on the Football Pitch

*Dance – seductivo molto sexio!*

WOMEN

    MEN

Hand on chest,

    Pushing head and neck outwards

closed eyes and

    with Adam's Apple jerking up and

expression of deep

    down. The men hold sticks which

trance, as in love –

    they brush against themselves;

making at the critical

    very seductive.

Moment!

    (Now read it backwards!)

'. . . another fantastic dance is known as "Falata". It originates from Nigeria when Muslims passed through Sudan on the "Hadj" to Mecca. Some of them settled in Sudan and became cultivators.

The Falata is a wild dance in which men leap around in a circle jumping to a war-type cry as they bash sticks together to the accompaniment of a frenzied drummer beating a tin can.

Other instruments I recorded were the Kiata trumpet from Chad. This once again sounded more Egyptian than Sudanese – the breathing technique was Egyptian.

The recording I have is excellent and in my Mass it ought to be heard in a dance-type interlude in which I shall bring in a battery of percussion instruments like a Scottish Reel twirling around the Kiata – a technique not unlike Benjamin Britten's "This ae nighte" from his "Serenade" for Tenor, Horn and Strings. The Kiata can be the "ostinato" – "This ae Kiata!"

Today Saleh and I went off to find a Greater Kudu Horn, now very rarely heard. At one time it was blown to gather men together for war or for a lion hunt. In a neighbouring village we managed to trace a very dusty one hanging up in a hut and with the assistance of the Shirtie and Omda a lion hunting party was organized. This proved not very successful as there aren't any lions left in the neighbourhood! Nevertheless, I recorded what I could and the following translation was given me by my dear friend Saleh to whom I shall be devoted forever. He had tears in his eyes as we said goodbye in the market place, and as I left by truck for Nyala his parting words were: "You will write me often Mr David?"

There he goes, I thought as I waved goodbye, of course I will write, in fact I'll even include his name in *Salaams* alongside Basil Ali Hateem and the Shaikh of Bahrain. That is the least I can do.

### Lion Hunting Songs from Zalingei
#### Translated by Saleh Adam Gasim – October 1969

We are calling for courageous men to go fighting.
We are following the trace of the lion.
We are never frightened.

When we are running after the lion –
Now it is in front of us.
All Gentlemen be courageous to kill it.
All the courageous men are after the lion and our
    houses are completely empty.

The courageous men are really Men.
The frightened ones are like women because they
    are not able to follow them.
We are the people of the Tribe [Fur]
We want our families to produce boys not girls
    for fighting.

Al Yum Yum'na!
Al Yum Yum'na!

It is our day!
It is our day!
Today we shall drink the blood of a courageous
man.*
Let us go inside our houses not to be blamed by
the women.
We can go inside our houses because they blamed
us before killing the lion.
It is our day – today we shall drink the blood of a
lion!

I remain your faithful servant,
Fried Eggs 26.10.69 . . .'

When I got back to Khartoum from West Sudan it seemed the whole world was nothing but one big problem. First of all I was told by the Sudanese authorities it would be impossible for me to continue south following the course of the Nile through to Uganda. Apparently 'The Sudd' was yet another prohibited area. Secondly my application to the Arts Council of Great Britain for extra finance had been turned down and I received a letter from them saying:

'. . . your present tour of North Africa has been carefully considered by the committee which advises the Council on its Awards to Artists Scheme, and I am sorry to have to tell you that an award was not recommended . . .'

At the time the words 'tour of North Africa' angered me so much I wrote back and advised them that I thought there ought to be an 'Arts Council Expeditionary Force' by camel from Tangiers to Chad. At the bottom of the letter I remember drawing a whole string of camels and imagined the 'Awards to Artists Schemers' trying to do what I had done

---

* A difficult translation to explain, but as I understand it from Saleh it refers to the courageous man who has been wounded in his attempt to kill a lion. The blood from his own body is sacred if it has been drawn by the lion in the fight, it also has something to do with the cleansing of the wound – but this musn't be taken too literally.

wearing nothing but their bowler hats! In retrospect (no hard feelings) I would like to thank the Arts Council for their subsequent help with funds in preparation for the first performance of *African Sanctus*.

In Khartoum, however, it seemed the only thing to do was to turn a disadvantage into an advantage, buy myself more time and hope that the Ministry of Guidance would change their minds and grant me a permit to go through 'The Sudd'.

S O.

Turning the whole axis of my journey into another shape, I decided to go east and record music from the tribes of the plains near the Red Sea hills. The shape of my journey then became a Cross with a new meaning.

*Journey to East Sudan – November 1969*
'. . . the success of my journey to East Sudan depended on whether or not I could find Shaikh Mohammed el Amin Tirik – a "Cambridge Man" but now, after the death of his late father, Nazir (head) of the Hadandua people who roam about the plains with their cattle.

He was a difficult man to trace.

On arrival at Kassala a message came by camel from Woga Wells. Shaikh Mohammed had apparently sent for me and so it was so. When I arrived at his Palace in Aroma I found him holding Court (Muglis) amongst his Elders, father's retainers, servants and so on.

He looked at me with bloodshot eyes and leaning forward on his stick, his turban piled high on his head, he suddenly said in very clear English:

"Oxford, or Cambridge?"

"Royal College of Music, Your Highness," I replied.

We broke for breakfast and I began to explain what I was trying to do. Shaikh Mohammed listened and it seemed we were going to be very good friends. You can usually tell by the way another listens – his bloodshot eyes became far removed, then he spoke: "I am not a Cambridge Man you know, I am actually a Cantabian – Trin . . . ity College." And that was my initiation into the Hadandua Tribe! He not only created me a Brother Shaikh, by giving me the traditional clothes worn by his people, he also introduced me to the Hadanduan way of life. Together we recorded a very rare collection of music from East Sudan which includes cattle songs, prayers of the Elders, war dances and the war drums which belong to his family, recitations of the Quran in the prayer schools and even the prayers of his personal Prophet or spiritual leader.

Life here is totally different from the Marra Mountains. In character the Hadandua are very warlike – for centuries they have had to protect their cattle and grazing grounds, particularly water wells. Their music is slow and sad – the one principal instrument used is the Bazen-kop, not unlike an ancient Egyptian lyre.

Bazenkop music of the Hadandua has a marked and descriptive quality about it. Descriptive of the hardships which they encounter. Each tribe has its own particular set of "tunings" and the instrument is usually played solo without any accompaniment from the voice. To the uninitiated it sounds like a bad guitar-player fiddling about! But if you live with these glorious people you learn to slow down and the simple tunes (or fiddles) that one hears by the light of a fire at night with the accompaniment of the camels chewing soon becomes as moving as the journey you have made by day.

My position now is somewhere north-east of Kassala in the middle of a vast, flat, arid plain.

They have given me a bed of matted rope and even when I am lying down I can see that the earth is round – my horizon is like a shimmering lake – there seems to be a huge sea stretching away like a flood. Bushes, very low, look swamped in the mirage and the whole vision is dotted with moving things. These are the cattle of the Hadandua and they move in hundreds across the plain as they are brought to the wells for water.

I am living in a tent with dried intestines hanging down above my head.

It is difficult to write because the wind keeps rustling the paper, blowing sand in my face.

Now, as evening approaches, the lake becomes a deep golden colour and I can distinctly pick out the soft line of the distant Red Sea hills.

The Hadandua are a branch of the Beja Tribes who spread up the Eastern side of Sudan. They are still nomadic and depend upon watering holes for their cattle; these are numerous and stretch out across the plains known as "the Gash". It is unfortunate because in my "village" a woman died last week in childbirth and the whole encampment is in mourning. The Shaikh of the village has told me that his people will only sing on the seventh day of mourning but not until then.

Sometimes I can see all the women setting off in a line – they shimmer in the sunlight as they fling their arms in the air, moving in a line to a spot where they let out piercing wails. They cry and fall to the ground with grief. Of course, I cannot go to them – this part of Sudan has very strict Muslim laws and the men are completely separated from the women by day. A man can only go to his wife by night.

All around me is a deep smell of cattle and the men have an odour which makes you feel very sick at first. Their hair is matted with dung and they have it piled high with long tresses down the back of their necks. This protects them from the sun. I believe Rudyard Kipling once described them as "Fuzzy Wuzzies".

I think they are like Gods in the sunlight. Their swords glitter at their sides. The Hadandua are so different from the Fur and in many ways they are very close to one's true vision of Arabia.

The sun governs the hour of the day and when it drops it is dark.

If I walk away from my tent I am soon swallowed up in silence that makes my ears buzz. It is still – and the vast emptiness of the desert fills me with a feeling like heaven and death. Surely it is as silent as this when one dies?

Praying is part of life and I am allowed to give the Muezzin five times a day; they like the way I call the people to prayer very much. Prayer comes naturally and is accompanied by the washing of feet and hands. One looks forward to this. I do not think it wrong that I should pray with my hosts – nor do they, in fact it is a wonderful feeling to pray in line with such men.

As I write to you, a little circle of mystified faces has gathered at my feet. They do not understand how anybody can write like I do. I only hope my readers will!

Thank God for such a world as this. Music is like a wound that never heals . . .'

## The Love Song

It is very rare for the Hadandua to sing about love. Shaikh Mohammed explained that the music of his people was usually associated with war. When I played him the Love Song, which I happened to record one night out in the desert, he became very moved and said that the singer had a wonderful gift. He said it was obvious from the song that there had been peace for some time in the area from which the singer came. He thought that area was probably the Red Sea hills.

It was near midnight when a cattle boy came in to my encampment riding on his camel. Quite unexpectedly, after drinking coffee, he began to play the Bazenkop which he had been carrying on his journey. Very discreetly I approached him and accustomed him to the sound of his voice which he was astonished to hear for the first time coming out of my 'Magic Box'.

In *African Sanctus* the Hadanduan Love Song can be heard accompanied by a short piano sonata I composed. The movement further evokes the musical and spiritual relationships which I have tried to conjure up in an Interlude during the Mass, expressing my love of music from both the East and the West.

After the Love Song you can hear the sound of tiny bells ringing in the desert. Shaikh Mohammed told me that they are part of a very ancient custom of his people which signifies the birth of a new-born son. The ringing bells help the infant to become strong and fearless and protect him from the 'Evil Eye'.

The Love Song, piano sonata and bells ringing in the desert are a poignant moment for they not only signify the birth of a new-born son in the East of Sudan, they also represent the birth of Jesus Christ who was born of the same simplicity, love and courage.

Here is a literal translation of the Hadanduan Love Song translated by Shaikh Mohammed el Amin Tirik in 1969.

## Love Song

When she passes by you she gives such an aroma
    that it never leaves even when you are asleep.
If when you wake in the morning and move,
You have to be careful not to move too much
    otherwise it might even come out of your own
    breath.

If you love her, other people will smell it
    and men will fall in love with her, and women
        will get jealous.
She has excelled other girls in all qualities and her
        hands,
    when she is walking, are so admirable that
    one can *not* resist the desire to touch them
    as if she were carrying a gold stick.*

Why do you give a colourful cotton cloth to her
        mother
    as though you were giving the remains of food to
    a she-dog?
Why, you ought to have given her mother clothing
        of pure silk
    knitted with gold thread.

Her wedding train is something that is to be
        respected,
like a ship that is filled with courageous men who
    are

---

* This sentiment refers to a phrase in the Quran in which the Prophet Moses was said to have such a mysterious stick that when he moved it, it destroyed all his enemies.

prepared to defend their comrades in the front
line.
(Verse repeated)

Those white teeth – would they never be dirtied by
any material,
Never lose the front smile by missing them.
(Verse repeated)

Her fingers are *so*, that when I shook hands with
those rings
that should not have been worn to add beauty
to those smooth
flexible fingers as though they were created
without bones,
I suddenly became senseless.

## The Case of the Missing Sword

'. . . This amusing incident happened only yesterday at the Muglis
when I was sitting with Shaikh Mohammed el Amin Tirik at the
morning hearing. Many Hadandua had gathered to present their
various problems and complaints. As Shaikh Mohammed translated
the complicated proceedings into English I could hardly believe my
ears – do bear in mind that it's 1969!

Complainant A reports that he has been told by his Uncle B that a
sword which C has *is* the sword of the late father of D that has been
lost for about forty-four years.

The complainant would like his sword back.

Now A has actually seen the sword with C because C has pawned
the sword about six months ago with A's employer D.

C, when asked, says "It is true, I had a sword which I bought from a
merchant who is present. Being my sword, having bought it of course,
I had the right to pawn it and actually I have sold the sword to my
brother who doesn't know where the buyer is."

Merchant E when asked to explain said:

"About twenty-two years ago, after the First World War, a certain Hadandowi whom I had never seen before and never saw again and could not recognize if I did see again, came into my shop and bought goods to an amount of three and a half pounds. He asked me to keep the goods and sword for a short while and walked out. He came back shortly and said that he couldn't find the man from whom he expected the money. He asked me to let him have the goods and sword, saying that he would bring the money after three days. He swore by Allah that he would bring the money. I said to him 'Don't swear by Allah, take your sword and leave my goods.' He pleaded that he was in very bad need of the goods so in the end he took the goods and left the sword, saying that he would come back in three days, but I never saw him again.

"Six years ago I sold the sword to my sister's husband's brother because no one claimed it and I don't use swords."

Shaikh Mohammed asked the merchant why he hadn't reported the case earlier?

The complainant again repeated that he had never seen the sword and couldn't recognize it if he saw it, but that he wanted it back.

"How do you think the sword which you have not seen and could not recognize if you saw it, came to be with either the merchant or with your Uncle?" asked Shaikh Mohammed.

"My brother forgot my sword at some wells, the Woga Wells. Two Gallaheen had been seen around that area," replied the complainant.

"Then why didn't you report it to the police or to the Shaikhs when you saw the Gallaheen?"

"We were so ignorant of such things at that time," said the complainant.

"When was the last time you saw the sword with the merchant's sister's husband's brother and how long ago?"

"About five years ago."

"Then why didn't you report it then?" questioned Shaikh Mohammed.

The complainant replied: "I was too busy with my animals."

## Interludes

After the case had been discussed for about five hours, Shaikh Mohammed asked *me* what I thought he ought to do with them?

I wasn't quite sure because I was far too busy trying to fathom it all out in my notebook. Tactfully, however, in the end it was suggested that both complainant A and merchant E should pay a fine of ten shillings each to Shaikh Mohammed for having wasted his time . . . !'

## Red Herrings

From Aroma I bought a third class railway ticket and went to Port Sudan hoping to find examples of fishing music on the Red Sea. The whole journey was a disaster.

'. . . Dear Trust – continued,

The dust flies in every direction, children scream and the women, like black crows, balance them on their laps shaking them up and down.

It's just like a cattle truck – all the shutters are down and the smell from the lavatory is heavenly!

Like an impregnable storm-trooper-train we wind northwards across the battlefield of a wintry, desolate desert.

I am rubbing shoulders with a tribesman whose sword keeps digging into my thigh. He leans forward and spits monotonously – his hair is wild and hangs in tresses down his neck, it is caked in *waduc* (boiled cattle fat). We are jogging along.

Last night at midnight the train arrived at Aroma station in pitch darkness. I couldn't see a thing. Not even a light at the station. In the gloom I climbed up, picked my way through bodies scattered everywhere, and eventually came upon a couple of wooden seats which were occupied by one snoring, white-clad figure. Being Male I thought this was a "bad show" and certainly wouldn't have been allowed on the "Southern Region", so I politely asked the fellow to "budge up". All was quiet until I could stand it no longer – I swiped him with my head scarf.

He leapt up and we were just starting to have a row when up came Shaikh Mohammed el Amin Tirik swinging a bottle of local sherry.

Miraculously the fellow squirmed into the corner of his seat and said not a word.

The last I saw of my noble host Shaikh Mohammed was when the train began to gather momentum – he couldn't get the door open so he stumbled over all the bodies and just as the speed of the train was becoming dangerously fast he leapt off, bottle in hand, white-flowing garments flashing in the wind. His teeth showed up in the night as he ran alongside the train still holding on to the door handle. We shouted at each other, but the train overtook him and he finally fell backwards into the night. The train whistled as I settled in my hard-fought-for place. Luckily I was wearing my Hadanduan clothes which helped pad the slats of the seat. It was like a horse-box. I felt sad leaving behind my honourable friends.

There is a woman sitting on the floor beside me being milked by her child – I don't know if I'm supposed to look or not but really she is very voluptuous!

It is now midday and the scenery has completely changed, becoming very rugged as we pass through the northern extremities of the Red Sea hills. I shall shortly hitch a ride by truck to Suakin, an old fortress town which once belonged to the Ottoman Empire on the Red Sea. It is here that I hope to trace musical influences which may have come up from the trading routes of the Indian Ocean.

Most courageously, I am your bad writer and most faithful friend.

P.S. I don't quite know who my friends are? . . .'

'. . . My lift to Suakin has led me slightly off the beaten track to Tokar and it seems as though I'm barking up the wrong tree, as I am in the middle of the desert again!

"No fish in the sand" they said at Tokar in all seriousness.

So tomorrow I shall walk to Suakin and search for an old fisherman called Hassan Bauday. In the meantime I have been invited to a wedding in Tokar by the District Commissioner . . .'

'. . . It was a modern affair with popular Sudanese music plus Western violins – HORROR!

Even so, to attend such an event is absolutely charming.

All the women and girls were at one end, dressed in heavenly deep butterfly colours amongst the twinkling lanterns.

One in particular was the One whom I would have died for – she was wearing a pale mauve shawl with silver brocade around her face.

Her beautiful white eyes shined in the night – I would fall down, for I felt so much for her light.

Suddenly she began to sing a solo and all around her the butterfly colours clapped and sang in a chorus. Little girls began to dance in front and the men raised donkey sticks and clicked their fingers in agreement!

Luckily, I had my tape recorder going and using it as an excuse for an advance upon my butterfly darling, I advanced behind two microphones. I was dressed in my Hadanduan tribal clothes.

I stood before her and recorded what she sang and begged for air to breathe and space in which to fly because I could not, as I do not have any wings.

Behind me the little girls danced and behind them the Bridegroom raising his clicking fingers made jerking motions at his fellow men who clasped him like Romans around the forearms.

"HEE YOY YOY YOY YOY YOY YOY YOY YOY YOY" cried the butterflies, their eyes gleaming in the torch-light.

I would jump or beg God to relieve me of my passions for I know I do not belong – but please somebody will you tell me where I *do* belong because I love my butterfly without doubt, much better than all the conservative whisperings of my English, Mini-skirted, Short-breasted, Truthful-friends.

I STOOD, breathless in hopeless loss with my microphones and tape whizzing round and round. Lost in traditions unknown to me, looked upon as a foreigner – a visitor – a strange world to look upon in traditional Hadanduan clothes – so I spoke.

I said to the romance before me –

"Gameela" which means beautiful.

She started back and hid her lips from my sight behind a curtain of mauve. Just two staring eyes stared.

I withdrew, pulled at the elbow by the District Commissioner who explained in breathless tones that I must only look –

"She knows from your looking," he said, "It is an insult to speak."

I sat back on the chairs provided, adjusted my head-dress and put away my microphones.

But between her and me lay a thousand years of difference and colour. I saw her all the time – she stood out from all the others and I felt sick with longing.

We left, the District Commissioner and I.

Now I have no one except this page and you Miss Williams who will, I am sure, think nothing except thin air . . .'*

'. . . The only fishing music I have found on the Red Sea came with the help of an introductory letter to Hassan Bauday.

After a race against stormy weather and a thirteen-hour ordeal tossing up and down in a tiny fishing boat about five miles out to sea from Suakin, during which time the fishermen never stopped bringing up terrible, yellow, half-pukey-fish – with my tape recorder under my knees protected by the salt-coated sackings of fish nets – I heaved and cursed every wave that slashed across my "Magic Machine". Those bloody fishermen never sang a single note!

Finally Bauday, who asked for £5, arranged exactly what I wanted in the calm of the harbour. As expected, there *is* a tremendous similarity in tone and rhythm between Red Sea music and the music of the Indian Ocean . . .'

## Sudden Rescue

Having hitched in an aircraft with a doctor of medicine (with letters after his name) I returned to Khartoum from the Red Sea, once again excited and stimulated by all that I had seen and done – but the situation had not improved.

'. . . my application for a permit to go through "The Sudd" has finally

* Potato !

156

been rejected. Unable to do any broadcasts in Khartoum I cannot earn any money, also unable to pay for an air fare with Sudanese currency – plus the fact I am stuck in Khartoum with fifty Sudanese pounds in cash which cannot be used. I have also been advised to leave Sudan rather sooner than later.

I have pleaded with every Ministry, had endless discussions – all a waste of clock. Today I even approached the Minister himself for permission to go as far south as Juba but was advised yet again to return *bukra* (tomorrow). It seems hopeless.

I fear all my films and tapes might be confiscated as I stupidly tried to sell copies of them to the radio station. Am making every effort to get them flown out through the good hands of B.O.A.C. representatives in Khartoum. Thinking I was going down to the Customs Shed I accidentally walked into the Anglican Bishop's Office by mistake today where I met the Anglican Clerk's Secretary and a "Missions to Seamen" fellow from Port Sudan. Having explained who I was and what I was trying to do they informed me that if I was searching for the music of Sudanese refugees, there were literally thousands of them waiting for me in Uganda!

With these two prophetic words "Sudanese refugees" I suddenly feel an almighty burden lifting off my shoulders. The faster I get out of Sudan and into Uganda the better, despite the disappointment of not being able to go through "The Sudd". In my excitement and with the prospect of having to become a refugee myself, I told the clerk in the Anglican Bishop's office about my plans for writing a Mass combining the Christian and Muslim faiths – he was shocked.

"Why not use the Coptic Mass?" he asked with a saintly expression.

"Because," said I, not quite knowing what to say next, "because I am more of a musical journalist and I like the thought of flinging Latin and Arabic together."

"Who wins?" laughed the "Missions to Seamen".

"God I suppose" said I and smartly left for the Customs Shed who said –

"Go to the Ministry of Commerce" who said –

"Go to the Ministry of National Guidance" who said –
"Go to the Bank of Sudan" who said –
"Go to the Customs Shed."
So I didn't!
Instead I went to see Sean O'Fahey at the University of Khartoum who said –

"We find your recordings not only of the highest significance and importance to our research, but of the highest originality. We feel that 'The School' (S.O.A.S.) will pay you handsomely for such material, therefore, we suggest you go and see the anthropologist Andrew . . ."

I regret I would not want to do the anthropologist an injustice but I cannot spell his name.

I left my recordings with the "phonetic department" so that copies could be made before they were finally flown out by an Armenian refugee, c/o B.O.A.C., who was emigrating to Montreal, stopping off in London en route.

P.S. I have decided that the Arts Council of Great Britain Expeditionary Force will leave Folkestone for Tangiers and Chad on 1 January, 1970 . . .'

There I was alone, wondering how to get to Uganda, standing on the banks of the Nile gazing at Kitchener's Gunboat near the Old Palace, not far from the Post Office –

'. . . "POST OFFICE!" I shouted, dashing down the avenue of acacia trees, hoping that there might be a letter from the R.V.W. Trust. Puffing and panting Fanshaouwee (Sudanese spelling) enquired if there had been any mail for him.

Wonders will never cease, a telegram was handed over the counter.

DAVID FANSHAWE
PO BOX 50
KHARTOUM
ONE HUNDRED POUNDS PAID YOUR BANK HYTHE TODAY
    WILLIAMS

Your generous news comes with such relief and gives me heart that my invaluable research *is* worthwhile and that old R.V.W. *must* be smiling down watching me sweating it out day after day!

I only hope I cause you no real bankruptcy and that you are not saying to yourselves "that bloody idiot Fanshawe!"

Because I am going to return with something worth thousands of delights and you are all going to hear them.

Thanks to Miss Williams R.V.W., all tapes and films have left Sudan and tomorrow I fly direct to Entebbe – to continue the search amongst Sudanese refugees on the Sudan-Uganda border and when I return I shall take Miss Williams out to lunch and AFRICA!

So tonight I'm gin'd – I can fly! I can fly!!

N.B. How do you eat a German sausage in the Sudan?

You get on the Lufthansa flight at Khartoum and fly to Entebbe – goes every Friday night and by God I could do with one of these air hostesses –

But I sit and they pass by and all I get is a sausage for looking . . .'

Quite impossible to publish in this Epistle but clearly visible in the original letter you can see, at this point, a yellow-brown mustard blob which the Defendant smeared on the letter saying: Mustard of the Sausage – Taste it and see!

'...PASSING OVER THE EQUATOR FOR THE FIRST TIME IN MY LIFE!
OH FOR A BIRD TO CELEBRATE!
MISS WILLIAMS, MISS WILLIAMS, R.V.W., R.V.W.!
OH FOR A BIRD ON THE LINE!

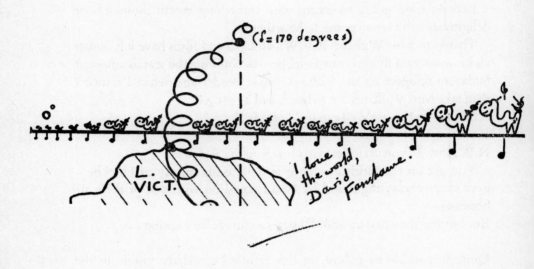

I EQUATE AT THE LINE!
"CROTQUAVE RECORDIO"=170 DEGREES!
FROM THE SKY I LAND
HERE WE GO
OH FOR A BIRD ON THE LINE!!!'

## Notes Only

'. . . Entebbe Airport – wet and cold – joined queue through customs organized by beautiful uniformed East African Airways hostess in light fawn suit – stockings and splayed skirt!

Slept the night under a market stall in Kampala – had wallet stolen – luckily no money.

Nelly, who works for B.O.A.C., took me to Makerere University and invited me to stay – suddenly found myself in an Indian community in Kampala and within hours had been introduced to Scottish Professor Gourlay.

Together, Gourlay and I drew up the following plan after dinner and now – EXECUTION!

Leave Kampala Tuesday, start work amongst the Lakeside people of Samia Bugwe (unexplored area), journey north to the Busoga people and Lake Kyoga, continue north to Gulu and Acholi Tribe (a branch of the Luo) hitch through the bush to the Sudan-Uganda border, (where the refugees can be found in special camps) – travel west to the Congo and back east mostly on foot, across Karamoja to record the very remote Karamajong – return to Kampala – catch bus to Nairobi, return Nairobi/London on charter flight.

In other words – very busy . . .'

# X

# *Et in Spiritum Sanctum*

The South of Sudan is one of the most important areas of the Nile both geographically and ethnically (horrid words), for it contains the roots from which so many Nilotic peoples have their origins. 'The Sudd' is perhaps the pivot of African culture on the eastern side of the continent, and in 1969 was facing a period of considerable turbulence due to the Christians of the South wanting independence from the Muslims of the North – that is how I understood it anyway. Because of this I was determined to record whatever music I could find from the refugees who were, at the time, fleeing into Northern Uganda.

My letters were full of torment since I too faced heavy opposition from the Ugandan authorities while trying to obtain permits to enter the refugee camps. I also found that many educated Ugandans were unsympathetic towards my ideas of musical preservation; having been on the move for so long the strain began to show.

'... MUSIC MEANS:

Mosquowtoes, banana trees, papyrus swamps, rain clouds, wild animals, drunken Nilots, aeroplane tickets, expulsion, ships, wooden canoes, crucifixes, beer parties, camels, malaria, theft, visas, sandstorms, frogs, impassible roads, broken-down trucks, Pepsi Cola, funeral parties, worn razor blades, donkey sticks, T.A.B. injections, rubber Dunlop shoes, blazing sun, fertility rites, big round breasts, teeny weeny shrivelled breasts, fish, lion hunts, Greater Kudu Horns, Snakes, Anthropologists, Italian Fathers, Community Development Officers, corned beef, jail, water pills, groundnuts, sorghum, milk, eggs and powdered bananas, "short calls and long calls", spears, madness, flat batteries, drunken Shaikhs, dirty pants, Polish immigrants, Post Offices and last but not least music means – SUDANESE REFUGEES and if any

162

of them sings "Lead Kindly Light" or "All Things Bright and Beautiful" (beautiful they may be) I'll bash 'em on the head with my microphones.

At this point I must go and wash my feet – the smell is too awful and the mosquowtoes are worse than ever before, they've even found a way into my mosquowtoe net.

It's really a beautiful bog and I have quite decided to compose a "Frog Symph". Did Haydn do one or didn't he?'

'. . . I now write from the Sudanese refugee settlement area called Onigo which is in Madi District in the extreme north-west corner of Uganda.

It is quite beautiful here, and the rolling country gradually slopes down to the Nile, which spreads out amongst floating islands of papyrus swamps some eight miles across the Nile Valley.

I am within sight of the high plateau of Southern Sudan and it is now the cotton-picking season. All the refugees are busy in the fields; however, I am hoping that a gathering tonight will prove successful musically.

I am very tired now and the fight I have had to get all this music has taken every ounce of persuasion, bullying, charm, waiting, energy, calm and even *more* persuasion than I possess.

Today I have just walked up from a small village on the Nile to the refugee camp. It was an exhausting walk, about ten miles, and on the way I met a student wearing a brightly-coloured shirt with a high collar. He had a very polished bicycle and didn't seem at all interested in the traditional music of Madi.

I approached, covered in red dust, and followed him towards some mango trees into the long grasses – I was at the time searching for a refugee called Lazaro who might have helped, but a conversation like this only reveals the unfortunate suspicions one can come across in Africa today.

ME  Good afternoon.

HE  Yes? (said slowly).

ME  Do you by any chance know where Lazaro is? I met him yesterday and he said he would meet me but hasn't turned up. He said he lived somewhere near here.

HE  (Pause) For which purpose is your motive for planning such a meeting?

ME  Well you see he is a friend.

HE  Your motive is?

ME  Perhaps I should introduce myself – how do you do. I am David Fanshawe from London, I'm a musician and I am here hoping to record traditional music in the refugee camp. This is my Government Pass. I have no motive except that Lazaro said he would gather some of his friends together tonight and sing me some traditional songs.

HE  Then if you want songs it is more advantageous for you to remain for your songs on records. (Pause)

ME  But couldn't you please tell me where Lazaro is? I know he's here somewhere.

HE  What makes you believe so?

ME  Because he told me he was a refugee from Onigo Camp and his home was somewhere near here.

HE  Then the political issue is one of discrimination and I don't think you have any right as a colonialist to intrigue in our villages.

ME  Look . . .

HE  Yes Man I can see you (he interrupted).

ME  I am a composer from the Royal College of Music, I'm not interested in politics – all I have come to do is record a few songs which Lazaro said he would sing. Can you please tell me where he is?

HE  That is not a question, it is a demand and I do not obey strangers.

ME  Well DON'T!

HE  Go off – go off! We don't want your white skin here (he sneered).

Five minutes later the same student approached me again, this time half riding, half shuffling on his bicycle – it seemed as if he couldn't keep away.

ME  Look here, I simply wanted to ask you for your help. (Pause)

HE  That's better Man, if you ask another's help then it can be given. (Another pause)

ME  I am trying to find Lazaro, does he live near here?

HE  That's calmer Man, you see we want to help you but we cannot help if you shout and give us orders.

ME  Then can you please tell me if you know Lazaro and if he lives here?

HE  (Stroking my arm in an ingratiating manner) Then why don't you go to those mango trees over there – see Man, that big one? (Pointing) Ask for him there.

In the end I found Lazaro just below the mango tree – visited him and his friends every day for a week but they never sang a note.

Sometimes I can hardly bear to live with my frustrations – but I've just heard about another refugee camp on the other side of the Nile to the west . . .'

## I Cross the Nile Again and Again

'. . . I crossed it in a flat-bottomed boat at a place just south of Nimule. The nearest I could get to my dream, the South of Sudan.

I had been walking for two days from Onigo and suddenly descended. Below the high ground lay a glorious view.

In the evening, water birds flew low over the misty waters and once again I heard the "song of the frogs at dusk". Across the stillness I could see islands of papyrus and water lilies just drifting down towards the marshes of "The Sudd". As I stood by the waters I felt things so vividly and longed to explore as the others had done.

What is it about the Nile?

Sometimes I feel I can move mountains.

Sometimes I stand with my Cap on my head, with endless song and glorious noises shivering down my spine. My life is full of Praise and my language is Music.

Sometimes I stand in the very place where "They" passed by and yet I know that I can *not* move the mini-skirt. I know that I can *not* belong to the crowds who stare at Windsor Castle.

> Notting Hill Gate and those lonely, lonely flats –
> How can one live in one room and be a one-
>     roomed failure?
> I have my mother and father,
> I have the College,
> And now I have Miss Williams and yet,
> The task is *so* huge.
> Please God save the water lilies
> And if the Dragonfly can fly,
> Why not I?

> I gazed across the still waters to the Mountains
> And I heard again the Final Song of my work.
> Is it a hero who stands?
> Or is it a Ham?

> I may only cross the Nile once more,
> I may never see "The Sudd",
> So I got into a flat-bottomed boat,
> And levered my way across to the West . . .'

## The Crux of the Matter

I remember with great affection one particular family of the Zande tribe who had fled from Yambio in 'The Sudd'. I met them by chance on the West bank of the Nile; they were Christian refugees.

It was getting dark as I came upon their very improvised homestead which had homely smoke rising from its centre. Having nowhere to go I approached, told them who I was and gave them a little dancing display. This time I was lucky. James, a charming boy aged about eighteen, seemed keen to help and it turned out that he had been to a Mission School near Juba before his family had fled from the South of Sudan.

'. . . Never have I met a more musical family. Each one of them either sings or plays an instrument and the instruments, apart from the clothes they stand up in, are their only possessions. They have a small metal-pronged "thumb piano", a little wooden xylophone they call a Marimba and a bottle they use as a drum by beating it on the earth.

James tells me they like to make up songs about events, particularly events which are going to become history to the generations after them. Recent events in their lives can hardly have been more dramatic and practically all the songs they sing are about their recent flight through the bush from their homeland to the safety of Uganda.

Despite the terrors they have faced, the songs themselves are very happy songs – more than happy, for they reveal a calm and philosophical acceptance of life and its problems which many Africans seem to communicate in their music.

They are Christians and the land around them is lush green – no longer desert . . .'

In *African Sanctus* you can hear the 'Song of Flight' harmonized with a setting of *Et in Spiritum Sanctum, Dominum et vivificantem* which simply means – I believe in the Holy Spirit, the Lord, the giver of life. I chose to set these words from the Creed slightly out of context because their meaning is virtually the same as that expressed in the 'Song of Flight'.

Also, I discovered the Zande family a long way to the north of the Acholi people whose music plays such an important part in the next two movements of *African Sanctus* – bearing in mind that the whole conception of the work, its composition and style, changes according to the geographical locality of my journey south from Cairo to Lake Victoria.

When listening to *Et in Spiritum Sanctum* I am reminded of the great work carried out by Christian missionaries in Africa. At the same time I am aware that a Christian way of life may not always be right for it brings with it many of the undesirable overtones of Civilization, as I understand it, which seem to bury many of the traditions behind tribal life and tribal law.

I am sure African leaders know this; certainly the missionaries themselves are very aware of it and would do anything to prevent traditional customs from dying out. But with Christianity, Education and Modern Communication, what was once cherished as law must inevitably change – many would say that this is progress.

I believe the World's destiny is predetermined by some kind of Force. I would not want to change what I see. I can only be grateful for the privilege of being able to see it in my time and of being able to Praise it as I feel it.

In the same way that one is trained to analyse Western music, I was analysing another kind of natural symphony going on in the background as the Zande family were singing. It could hardly have been described as 'background' for it was more 'foreground' if not 'allround' music – millions of frogs croaking, 'mosquowtoes' buzzing and the intoxicating night roar of Black Africa.

At last I felt I was really there!

### Song of Flight and Creed

I am praying with my whole mind,
The Virgin Mary was the one who was looking
    after Jesus my Saviour.

## Et in Spiritum Sanctum

I am praying to God.

  (Chorus)  We came footing with our children,
               We cannot die because of suffering.

Oh my Lord Jesus Christ and God
My Saviour and Deliverer,
My case is in front of you.
I am praying to God.

          We came footing with our children,
          We cannot die because of suffering.

I have been driven by Mundukuru,
I have been driven from my home.
That I am now walking in the bush like a wild
  animal.
I am praying to God.

          We came footing with our children,
          We cannot die because of suffering.

All the wild berries and fruits of the bush,
I have eaten them all.
We have been running through the bush like the
  wild animals do.
I am praying to God.

          We came footing with our children,
          We cannot die because of suffering.

For us men and for our salvation
He came down from heaven,
Was incarnate of the Virgin Mary
  by the power of the Holy Spirit,
And was made man.

          We came footing with our children,
          We cannot die because of suffering.

I believe in the Holy Spirit,
The Lord, the giver of life,
   who proceeds from the Father and the Son.
Together with the Father and the Son
   he is adored and glorified.

        We came footing with our children,
        We cannot die because of suffering.

He it was who spoke through the prophets.

        We came footing with our children,
        We cannot die because of suffering.

I believe in one, holy, catholic, and apostolic church.
I profess one baptism for the remission of sins.
And I look forward to the resurrection of the dead,
   and the life of the world to come.

        We came footing with our children,
        We cannot die because of suffering.

# XI

# *Crucifixus*

Having returned from the Zaire border, I hitched back to Acholi country in Northern Uganda where I was privileged to be taken to a 'Musical Club' in Gulu and went to record the famous 'Dingy Dingy' dance in which young Acholi girls are supposed to praise their warrior leaders and boy-friends. Now I fondly imagined a fantastic spectacle, and had I been Walt Disney, I might have got one. Instead, half a dozen eager young ladies appeared rather shyly at first, dressed in a uniform of blue and yellow.

Blue bras and yellow skirts!

Almost as soon as the dance had begun, like some bizarre curse put upon us, our activities were rudely interrupted by an almighty equatorial thunderstorm which broke up the celebration. Heavy tropical rains poured down and as I looked up into the blackness above I thought I heard voices crying out 'Crucify Him! Crucify Him!' My interpretation of the Crucifixus is a very personal one and is based on the mental conflicts I face in Africa personified in the violence of that storm.

Packing up my equipment I hastened into the Club House under a corrugated tin roof, and on entering heard strange, ethereal sounds emanating from the gloom inside. The sound of rain crashing down mixed with harp-like music coming from the back of the hut immediately compelled me to separate the microphones and prepare to record. Placing one microphone by the door to capture the full force of the rain I suspended the other over a wooden beam above the head of a man who happened to be singing. One of his songs, which I like to call the 'Rain Song', is perhaps the most beautiful I have ever recorded in Africa. Unfortunately there is no translation. I only hope that the extraordinary narrative he sings reflects in some way the past glories of the Acholi – his ancestors, rather than some mundane matter – but then what *is* mundane matter?

Several years later, remembering the 'Rain Song' and those familiar words of the Creed, words taken for granted – learnt by heart as a boy standing on a 'Chic Weed' – I composed the two narratives together, presenting an operatic culmination of ideas which depicts in the storm an atmosphere of strife and war with the cries of South Sudan piercing through. The whole effect leads on towards the ultimate glory of resurrection and hope in the everlasting life. It is as if an Angel triumphantly stills the forces of nature and reminds one of the story of Christ who was crucified under Pontius Pilate, suffered death and was buried; who, after three days, rose again from the dead according to the scriptures, ascended into heaven and became One with his Father – the Creator of all things.

> And he shall come again with glory
> to judge both the quick and the dead;
> Whose kingdom shall have no end.

The Crucifixus became the central climax of my work because it seemed to me that African music itself was being crucified. In the storm I was tormented and when I wrote to the R.V.W. Trust on the same night after the storm had subsided I wanted to betray myself and my innermost secrets, rather than have to admit that what I had come so far to find – the musical heritage of Africa – merely took place in a Club organized for such activities. In fact I wrote nothing at all about the 'Rain Song', the Club or my experiences at Gulu. Since then I have adapted my way of thinking and have learnt to accept, with regret, the gradual disappearance of traditional folk music. An extreme example happened last year in Tanzania when I found mixed groups of musicians from many different tribes practising together wearing gym shoes and Chinese manufactured track suits. They were being instructed in the 'art of folk music' in an indoor football stadium alongside teams of acrobats and basketball players. I was even denied the honour of hearing them perform, let alone recording them, in case I might be an Imperialist 'stealing their culture'. What culture, I thought to myself as the door of the stadium was firmly shut in my face.

But in 1969, after the storm had ceased, the musician who accompanied himself on a seven-stringed 'Enanga' in the Club at Gulu finally emerged and sat with me on a wooden bench as we watched the 'Dingy Dingy' dancers begin their performance again. I think my guide said he was a policeman from Gulu Constabulary – certainly I believe he was a musical genius. I can tell you a lot about his instrument because he gave it to me as a present. Can you imagine a great violinist giving you his violin?

If you look inside the wooden frame of the Enanga you will see something rather touching – it's a Potato – on a thin strip of blue plastic there are some punched letters – LATIGO OTENG – and that is how I know his name.

## The Betrayal of Secrets

'. . . Funtington is not eight miles north-east of Bosham, it is four and three quarters. You take the lovely country road towards the circular wood on the Downs, carry on past Lavant House School for Girls until you come to Funtington.

You can't miss it, you lean out of the window of your car and in a clear and resonant voice you wake them all up shouting – "FUNT!"

You carry on to The Bull, sit down and have a delicious toasted cheese sandwich and half a lemon shandy. The locals will look at you, so you look at them and walk out into the buzzing summer evening and on you go to Petersfield where you remember what it was like and how you once sat in a thick hedge with your bicycle hidden waiting for Jane to ride by. Such Sussex evenings I do not forget especially now in my torment.

My heart remembers the hat she wore as she came out of Church and how I longed for her.

December to February in Acholi country should be the dryest time of year and yet the grasses are now so tall that you cannot see the women as they pass by to Chapel for Mass.

In Gulu I was able to stay with the American Brothers of the Sacred Heart.

Her shoulders were so smooth, her shoes so pointed and her steps as she walked kept pace with her father's. He knew what it was like to face "point-blank-gunfire". Her mother was off with the ladies of importance. I remember exactly the way she had her hair, parted down the middle with two front curls.

Then there were the days and days at the Aldershot Club – tennis tournaments, sandwiches and "all-whites" – until one day at the Tennants' Dance I was removed from my favourite perch, the piano, and was led out into the bushes beside the tennis courts – stripped and bashed up by five Sandhurst Cadets.

They had the razor, but forgot to bring a blade!

The leader's name was Peppa and he had no hair on his neck.

Two weeks later in New Oxford Street I became a junior assistant in a film company.

I fell in love with a Jewish girl and went to stay with Joel on a yacht in the South of France.

She lived in Spaniard's Row and one evening her mother said to me –

"David, I am very sorry, I know you will not understand it now, but Jill is eighteen and cannot be allowed to be with you alone any more."

That did it.

Slowly, like a heavy weight lifting from my head, every weekend I thumped and bashed on my piano in desperation with plenty of ideas but no technique or knowledge. I bashed out a hundred and twenty page Symphony but couldn't finish it. The second movement used a theme I got one day about a blind girl I knew and as I sat there playing it one night to some friends, I burst out crying and everybody became uncomfortably embarrassed just as anybody is going to be who reads this.

I speak my whole heart – why not? I only have Africa to speak to and you all seem so far away.

*Crucifixus*

No one knows what it's like to be possessed by horrid demons who push and push from within to attain soul and peace in music.

The effort – all that thumping nearly drove my parents round the bend.

We all know what it's like because if we know, then the spelling knows too.

To cast a spell takes years and people like me are going to be faced with the anguish – the No Recognition – the struggle to achieve perfection – the deep emotions which slice one up and make one run to the marshes, to the mountains or to the lands beyond the sea.

If only *someone* would follow me in a coffin wearing black gloves and a long, black veil into St George's Chapel where I once stood listening to The Choir and the footsteps of the Military Knights coming into Chapel.

I remember them saying "Tolls Down" – what does "Tolls Down" mean?

I cannot write a piano concerto, or an oboe quartet, or a string trio – I cannot write an electronic masterpiece in the style of BLOKHAUSEN.

I have to write things that bring other things together.

I have to write a Cross upon Africa exploring music from Cairo to Lake Victoria in the form of a Cross upon which is sung the Latin Mass.

Is this madness?

I insist that IF one takes – one MUST give back.

Just come and hear me on 18 May at the Queen Elizabeth Hall and you will hear something quite extraordinary.

I am going to greet all my friends, one by one, in a Symphony of Greeting and I will thank them for *all* they have done.

Such a beautiful echo of Mr Britten is in my head from his *War Requiem*:

> But the old man would not so, but slew his son, –
> And half the seed of Europe, one by one . . .
> . . . half the seed of Europe one by one . . .*

Repeat this verse over and over and over again . . .'

* 'The Parable of the Old Man and the Young' by Wilfred Owen.

# XII

# *African Sanctus*

*Exhibit Seven – dedicated to all the musicians who took part, in Africa,
in the first performance and in the recording, especially to those who neither
read nor write music.*

African people are used to celebrating all kinds of events – victories, the oncoming of rains, a fruitful harvest, a Day of Independence – you name it and they are there ready to celebrate. Therefore, it only seems natural that there should be a dance after the storm. The Sanctus movement is based on another famous Acholi dance from Uganda known as the 'Bwala Dance'. It is exactly what we all imagine African music to be, for it gives everybody a reason to sing, beat drums, eat, drink, fertilize and make merry – Members of the Jury.

Like all these things even the Bwala is dying out and when the Queen Mother visited Uganda in 1959 the dance was heard accompanied by a rather scratchy recording of Big Ben striking eleven o'clock. If it was like that in 1959 you can imagine how hard it was for me to gather a group of traditional Bwala dancers in 1969.

African Sanctus means Holy Africa and brings together the Sanctus from the Mass which is heard 'in concert' with my recording of a Bwala dance. It's rather like having an orchestra of a hundred African performers accompanying Western choir, percussion and pop group. I only wish the dancers could hear the combination for themselves as I know they would appreciate what had been done and would respond by joining in all over again! The principle behind such an *ngoma* is quite simply HARAMBEE! – the more the merrier. In many ways it is the same principle with a symphony orchestra, for one hardly ever specifies exactly how many violins should play. One's best intentions are usually defeated by the budget – not only in the concert hall, but these days in the bush as well.

This is how I eventually discovered a group of Bwala dancers who were willing to perform for a certain sum of money and of course, a lot of locally brewed beer.

'. . . I was lucky to meet on "the road" a Ugandan schoolmaster returning from Mbale to Gulu and he gave me a lift.

Now it happened that his village – the village where he was born – was a long way off from Gulu, out in the bush. On arrival the villagers were so pleased to see their "Son" we found no difficulty in arranging a Bwala dance.

When we returned two days later, of course, no one turned up. So a horn was blown, as is the custom, and sure enough on foot and on bicycles the men (once warriors) arrived carrying "their skins" in suitcases.

Behind the village "the team" discreetly changed, rather as I would change for a tennis tournament at the Aldershot Club.

Cigarettes were extinguished and by special request they even took off their wristwatches.

Harmless Bwala dancers then ambled forth and sat waiting patiently, adjusting their head-dresses which were magnificent.

Now I am not being cynical, I am simply trying to tell you exactly what I saw but you must understand I am secretly sad.

Drums suddenly began to beat, hastened on by one frantic Fanshawe who was far more concerned about the approaching clouds which would automatically destroy the photographic effect he hoped to achieve.

Then, suddenly, as if it had never stopped, the Bwala dance began. Immediately the "Westerners" became Africans again and the women with bouncing babies jiggled around in the middle yelling and screeching in impossible quarter constrictances.

About sixty sweaty dancers – twisting – pounding – diving – shaking with the sweat pouring in rivers down their black, black bodies, glistened in the blazing sun. The tall, lush, green grasses added the tropical colour of Africa to the background. So I pulled out my 135 Tele lens and shot 148 pictures within fifteen minutes. Grabbing a sugar cane pole, I tied the microphones on to an improvised "boom" and leapt into the middle of the dance, moving around in a cloud of dust kicked up by the stampede. The Bwala dancers went into a state of frenzy and rhythmical ecstasy praising Themselves, their Leaders and their Homeland – GLORIOUS AFRICA!

Time ticked away for the rest of the afternoon, long after dark, on invisible watches which remained hidden in suitcases. Many even had padlocks on them! . . .'

Why all this space?
Only thirty years or so?
If only I were longer
I might have seen more.

But the Doctor says
'You're lucky!'
The other Doctors say:

Sanctus, Sanctus, Sanctus
Dominus Deus Sabaoth.
Pleni sunt caeli et terra gloria tua.

Holy, holy, holy Lord God of
Hosts.
Your glory fills all heaven and
earth.

Hosanna in excelsis.
Benedictus qui venit in nomine
Domini.
Hosanna in excelsis.

Hosanna in the highest.
Blessed is he who comes in the
name of the Lord.
Hosanna in the highest.

Rattling their stones and
Secrets they repeat:

'Sanctus, Sanctus, Sanctus,
Dominus Deus Sabaoth.
Go and learn something
Oh my Friend,
Mr David –
Go and learn something.
HURRY!'

## Letters from Lake Kyoga – Uganda

My work on Lake Kyoga to the north of Lake Victoria went very well, and I was tremendously happy living in a small fishing village, having borrowed camping equipment from the Department of Agriculture and Fisheries in Soroti.

'. . . Father Cummock said, "Contact John Rogers in Soroti – *he* knows the lake inside out and will be a very great help to you."

So – He – Was!

When I arrived in Soroti from Gulu I went straight to John Rogers's office and was immediately invited to lunch.

"Do you want any fishing tackle?" he asked.

"No!" said I. "I'm from the Royal College of Music and I am here to record traditional fishing music from Lake Kyoga. I would be most grateful . . ."

Nile Perch was on the menu for lunch and after a delicious fruit salad we left in a Land-Rover complete with tent, mosquowtoe net, "Pal-ee-ARSE" (sleeping gear) and box of food supplied by the Fisheries Department.

"And good luck to you!" shouted John Rogers as he roared off.

I now write from inside the mosquowtoe net on the shores of Lake Kyoga in the middle of a funny little fishing village at night. I feel like Sir Samuel Baker – I think, except that I am minus a wife at present!

If only you benevolent musicians at home could see me now – extra loud farts down your rotten horns.

I am surrounded by belching frogs, more millions of mosquowtoes, thick papyrus swamps, the usual water-birds, more rotting fish and a small circular hut made of reeds and dried mud. I-AM-IN-IT!

Last night I thought the whole bloody lot was going to slip into the bog. I've never been in the middle of a more ferocious storm. I lay in my mosquowtoe net and remained brave. The lightning almost split me and the frogs apart and the thunder was much louder than the loudest *sfffz* in Mr Vaughan Williams's Fifth Symphony!

So here I am hoping that the fishermen will take me across the swamp, hoping that my slight fever will not get worse and that the steamy heat will not get any more humid. At midday it's so steamy that all the little fishing boats seem to emerge from a cloud which hangs over the lake.

I *am* that sort of mad "Bwana" you read about from time to time and I just wish these funking mosquitoes would shut up and choose one of the Pelicans instead. Oh it's a lovely night and all the noises make me very happy especially as I have today recorded *much* music which I will write about tomorrow when the light is a bit better . . .'

'. . . to start with it isn't really a swamp. The swamp part spreads out over a large area but in the middle there is a huge lake which is rapidly being developed by the Fisheries Department. It is "Scientific Fishing" and judging by the enormous specimens of Nile Perch I saw caught this morning, Mr Rogers and his assistants are being very successful.

Now where there is water there are no boundaries. It is this simple fact which makes up a fishing community. Fishermen don't fight and raid each other's fishing grounds, like the nomadic cattle-owning tribes, who depend on an unreliable water supply. A big fish can be caught almost anywhere close in or far out from the shore. That is why I have been able to find six different fishing communities in one village, six different languages and six different types of music. The peoples around Lake Kyoga and Lake Victoria consist mainly of the descendants of migrants from Southern Sudan. Some became cattle owners and cultivators, like the Acholi, others remained in one area like the Karamajong and some went further south, deep into the heart of the Rift Valley, like the Masai.

In recent months the word has spread that the "riches" of Lake Kyoga are far more rewarding than those of Lake Victoria, consequently many people who settled on the "big lake" have migrated north and have settled in fishing villages like this one, along the shores of Lake Kyoga, where I am now writing – although I never was much good at our language!

These are some of the fishing peoples I have recorded (hope the spelling is right):

The Jaluo – no instruments as they had to leave their drums behind in Kisumu. Their voices were very deep, rich and resonant.

The Teso play the "Akonga" – like a little hand xylophone with metal prongs. This instrument spreads right across the north of Uganda and into Sudan. It comes in many different sizes – Soprano, Alto, Tenor and "Bassos Akonga!" The Bassos Akonga makes a lovely resonating noise, almost as mellow as the lower register of a harp, and buzzes with vibratory seducement.

The Samia people have migrated north from Samia Bugwe on Lake Victoria. They have no instruments, having only recently settled on Lake Kyoga, but when I went fishing with them this morning they sang some splendid "work songs", rowing their canoes to the fish nets which had been left out overnight.

The Bakenye from Buganda also use the Bassos Akonga – I found their songs most charming – one in particular which says:

> If you borrow another one's bicycle,
> You must not look after it.
> But if it is your own, you keep it like a newborn
> baby.

What this has to do with fishing I'm not quite sure, except that everyone has one here – except ME. (I mean a bicycle not a baby!)

Then there are the Bunyoro who erected a fantastical thing across two banana trunks. I first set eyes on it as it was being bicycled from a neighbouring village. I couldn't for the life of me imagine how any banana trunk could be made to sound musical – but you see music works in strange ways. When a whole lot of thick and varying sized canoe boards had been laid across the banana trunks and little sticks had been stuck along the trunks between the boards – when hit by six players, the music was very bananary indeed! They call the instrument a "Madinda".

If you wish to know more about "xylophonocrity" do contact Dr Hugh Tracey who is the Director of the International Library of

African Music in Roodepoort, Johannesburg – he is the expert in such matters, I am the amateur!

The Busoga fishermen play real Jungle Rhythms on drums – knocking themselves out with head jerks – elbow back-handed belly flops – forward-striking (off-side) knee holds – high-hatted tripodic volley holds – spin-bowled (crawl bashers) and butterfly needles!

So you see the fishermen really make music and my musical jigsaw puzzle from Cairo to Lake Victoria rapidly gets filled in.

There is also an interesting comparison to be made between the music on the Red Sea and the fishermen of the lake. Both "Musicks" are alive and seem to encourage a rhythmical energy which is not generated amongst the cattle owners, nor amongst the nomadic peoples who travel along the recognized trading routes.

Does all this make sense?

P.S.    If a man wears no clothes he is NOT primitive.
If a man wears trousers and thinks he is not primitive,
    the chances are, he is.
But if a man wears trousers and takes them off
    in good company,
    then he must be very primitive.
TONIGHT I AM VERY VERY PRIMITIVE
    but unfortunately have no one to be primitive with.
No amount of Spirits can help me on that one . . .'

## John Weatherby and His Spirits

'. . . John Weatherby, wonderful hero and Friend of Africa, once told me on a mountain that he went up into the "high places" with his bearer and from behind a rock he heard the old men calling back the spirits of their ancestors as they sacrificed a goat on a huge fire. As they called to the spirits they swayed from side to side, and from a high cave in the moonlight the spirits replied in very faraway, high-pitched tones. John said he heard them quite clearly himself. The entrance of the cave was opened by two men who dared not look inside as the spirits were released everywhere. Although they were not seen they could be heard goading each other to jump across the fire and join their sons.

John says that in the "high places" there is no time of day – no north or south – just sunrise and sunset. They refer to the plains as "down there" and they fear those who may come back and steal their crops.

John Weatherby has been puzzling about these matters for many years and when he tells me about them he is deeply moved and when I sit with him I find that our two spirits are joined – it is almost as if I had spent all my life in search and now have found the man who searches with me amongst a lost people.

Ever since I was a boy I have made certain rituals and one is still continued. I gaze out of the window at home as my mother has her rest in the afternoon and I say:

"PUMP" said with clenched teeth.

"PUMP – what lies beyond the hills?" She then has to reply what she knows lies beyond the hills – but she doesn't, she says:

"The Sea" and I say:

"NOUGH!" which is a clenched NO, said very quickly as I sway from side to side reminding her of the answer to the question which is:

"FIRST THE LAND and THEN THE SEA."

And then I look at the cows in the field and my studio down by the stream and our funny old tennis court up on the hill and beyond the woods to the Priory and then the Romney Marshes and *then* the sea to the parts I love in Normandy to the Alps and beyond to the desert and Africa and then to the manuscript upon which I have been struggling, for it looks like the outline of a mountain surrounded by white space.

Out of the clouds as the rain falls I see a simple caption getting nearer and nearer and nearer –

DAVID FANSHAWE MET JOHN WEATHERBY
ON A MOUNTAIN IN AFRICA.

Perhaps it is a film?...'

### *Time*

Time is the Jumper – the starter – the faster
– the slower – the lonelier – the busier the time.

It goes wrong,
It makes excuses,
It isn't sometimes,
It's the girl of the moment –
It breathes and ticks.

It comes and goes with the Rainy Season.

Time is the End.

# XIII

# The Lord's Prayer

One day I was out fishing on Lake Victoria near the source of the Nile and as I paddled through papyrus swamps in a reed canoe I heard a soft wailing sound not very far away. Pulling the canoe into a tiny creek I waded ashore through the reeds and approached a solitary hut surrounded by banana trees and dense tropical vegetation.

# The Lord's Prayer

'. . . I approached slowly and guessed that someone lay inside.

Friends and relatives had gathered outside completely encircling the hut. They sat silently, many were crying.

Men with spades hacked at the wet soil – a hole big enough for a man?

It didn't seem an appropriate moment to enter but in Africa things are different and it is a custom for visitors to pay their respects on such occasions, bringing gifts to the owner of the home and his relatives. This I did and entered with my tape recorder.

I held the microphones in "closed" position and stood looking down upon the body of a dead fisherman. All the time I was conscious of my nervous and shaking hand which I had to control very hard knowing that this moment in sound would live forever. Sometimes it isn't easy to record human suffering.

I felt awkward.

At the fisherman's feet his wife knelt and at his head his mother cried and amid her anguish came the broken fragments of the most beautiful song – The Lamentation.

My thoughts wandered away for a moment in the stifling heat. Silently I said to myself the Lord's Prayer and was reminded of a Military Knight being buried in St George's Chapel – for we are all living NOW and OUR WORLD is getting smaller, and we have to work and pray together.

### Elegy for a dead fisherman

*ff*  I felt a huge – stone – building all round me and saw the man Lying in State, surrounded by a sarcophagus of marble.

*mp*  In the distance I heard The Choir singing.

*pp*  His mouth was tied up in a cloth.

*f*  The echo mingled and resounded with organ clashes that bounced off stone walls and vanished like shot from a mountain.

*mp*  Banners hung silently in The Choir – how I do remember their pale colours.

*pp*    His head flopped over towards his mother.

*f*    His body lay under stone in a musical place with the bones of Kings and Queens and upon his tomb was built his name,

*mp*    spelt in gold rings by angels who loved him.

*pp*    His frame was so small under the sheet.

*fff*    NO LIFE YET?

*mp*    Not even for a fisherman? He could not have been thirty years and yet,

*mf*    there he lay as still as tons of rock

*mp*    and yet,

*p*    I thought for a moment his shoulder was moving.

*pp*    His feet lay together – his beard was still growing and so his mother cried –

*ff*    'OH, my Son! OH, my Son! OH, my Son! OH, what is this? OH, my Son!'

*mf*    His wife cried also, great huge cries as if the world were Dead.

*p*    It was.

*pp*    He was all they had and yet,

*mp*    the frogs croaked and the Nana-Weed and Crod gurgled in the pool outside.

*mf*    In the afternoon the fisherman was carried out – his body was not yet stiff – his bones were still ready for another day's work and yet,

*pp*    his stomach was so ill that he had had to end.

*ppp*    NOTHING.

## Prayer for Strength

Good Lord deliver us.
Deliver us to do good amongst men
whether we are with them or over them.
Preserve and keep us whether we be of learning or
    not.
Good Lord.

If only we could see you good Lord,
If it were possible then perhaps it would be too
    easy for us to say
'I have seen The Lord'

Perhaps it is that we can NOT see you,
that we long to do so.
Good Lord deliver us as we were delivered long
    ago.

Let us speak and strike like the lightning that strikes
    this night.
Let us – if not US – then let ME
strike and STRIKE until my pen and chest be burst
    of ink and breath
to put it down – THAT which I have in my terrible
    head.
Let it come like the rain that falls this night.

Good Lord deliver us up above the swamp and
    water bug that floats –
flatly refusing to go anywhere but sideways.
If the Moon can rise – so can I.

Please God this night give us sleep above our
    thoughts
and peace if we deserve it.
If we do not – then send us to the bottom where
    no one lies.

I thank you for all I see and am able to do,
Please God I hope you have been hearing me,
because I am grateful to be alive . . .'

In *African Sanctus* the Song of Lamentation is followed by my setting
of the Lord's Prayer which is sung in English. It is an Offertory and
'soothing song' to the mother's lament and is harmonized in a style

which is popular today, not only in the West but in Africa as well. Many Africans know the words of the Lord's Prayer by heart, for they have as much meaning today as they did when they were first spoken two thousand years ago.

The Lord's Prayer is followed by the return to nature, to the wilds of Africa, to the sounds of a Masai *boma* (homestead) in the evening when mothers sing milking songs and men gather to praise what they have. Songs about cattle, sheep and goats, children, the green grass, the dry and the rainy seasons – in other words all men give thanks in their own way, and each song is in itself a Lord's Prayer.

### Masai Milking Song

I love you my favourite cow,
You provide us with everything,*
Your calves are always healthy, I really love you.
You were born from the biggest bull in the boma,
You give us the best kind of calves.

You expel poverty in the boma,
Cattle increase due to your breeding.
You are the soul of the homestead.
With you no poverty, no troubles, everyone is
    satisfied.
I really love you with all my heart,
You are my second God.

God is the giver of light,
The moon shines during the night and the sun
    shines during the day.
I always pray to God.

---

* As the Masai lady milks and sings she believes that the cow will give more milk with her encouragement. The song gives a special kind of feeling to the cow. If a mother doesn't sing, the cow may not give enough milk.

# The Lord's Prayer

## Song from Karamoja – Uganda

The river is bending the trees when it is in flood –
HOR HOR.
Omaniman flows to the West.
The river is bending the trees as it flows –
HOR HOR.

The river Kabilarmorok bending –
HOR HOR.
The river Lotenepusi –
HOR HOR.
Bending the river flows Hey-cookoh –
HOR HOR.

The river is bending Nyaawoi*
HOR HOR.
Bending Hey-cookoh –
The river Omaniman flows to the West.
It is entering the Lake,
It has entered the Lake –
HOR HOR.

## Turkana Cattle Song – Northern Kenya

When cattle are thirsty they moo,
because they are thirsty.
They thirst and they have many colours and long
    tails.
LOTODO!**

The saliva of the cows is on the pathway of the
    animals,

---

  * The collective noun of a particular type of tree known to the Karamajong, which the river always washes away when it is in flood.
  ** Refers to the shape of a one-horned bull standing somehow erect which the singers mime, showing the shape of the horn with their hands and arms – it is a symbol of ownership.

because they are thirsty.
Even when we take the cattle to graze early in the
    morning,
when coming back visitors follow us even into our
    bomas,
for they want our milk and blood.
We shall look after our animals until everybody
    has come to see them.
LOTODO! LOTODO!

We shall take them early in the morning to graze.
Even our enemies will start to wonder about our
    animals
saying 'HOH! HOH!'
The back of the cattle are looking yellow in
    the sunlight,
We shall look after them even until the rain comes
    to meet them.
LOTODO!

The spotted cows we shall look after you
even until the marriage comes.
You spotted cows migrate like elephants,
even when the owners of cows see the rain in
    another place
they shall move there.
When they took cattle to another place called
    Lolele
they stood there because they were satisfied.

Songs about cattle and the love that man shares with the fruits of the
earth are the very essence of praise. God is there in each and every song.
When I was very young I was taught to say:

> Our Father, which art in heaven,
> Hallowed be thy Name.

# The Lord's Prayer

Thy kingdom come.
Thy will be done,
in earth as it is in heaven.
Give us this day our daily bread.
And forgive us our trespasses,
As we forgive them that trespass against us.
And lead us not into temptation;
But deliver us from evil:
For thine is the kingdom,
The power, and the glory,
For ever and ever.
Amen.

God bless Mummy and Daddy,
Granny and Grandfather Fan,
Granny and Grandfather Mosse,
Aunty Patty and Uncle Pip,
Uncle John and Aunt Janetta,
Peter and Martin,
And Richard*
And all the people in the world
And God bless me.

This little ritual went on until I was supposed to have grown up – when
I went away to school.

Perhaps one doesn't say it out loud any more,
Perhaps one fails sometimes,
But one doesn't forget.

---

* Richard was my second brother who died aged four in Great Ormond Street Hospital after
nine plastic surgery operations for an internal malformation. The surgeon said at the time: 'Richard
did not die in vain, he has helped us, and other children will live.'

I was seven when he died and The Mouse has just reminded me of my immediate reaction when
she told me what had happened. I remember we were walking round the garden at Cedar
Cottage looking at the flowers.

'Oh Richard's so lucky – now he can go fishing with Jesus in Heaven.'

# XIV

# *Agnus Dei*

At last one is reminded of the very dust of Africa, the country's charm and humour, its gaiety and tragedy. Sadly, so many of the songs, rituals and dances of Africa have to end, for the world is changing. Again this is why I have felt the urgent need to preserve what I have been privileged to hear in Africa, and why I was inspired to write *African Sanctus*.

In the Agnus Dei, I reflect on the Sanctus Journey and all the feelings I have for my work in the bush. If one recording were to sum up those feelings I would choose the Luo Ritual Burial Dance from Western Kenya which pays tribute to a fallen warrior. The dance itself seems to signify the burial of African tradition, which brings me back to *you*, Members of the Jury and those present at the scene of this Trial for it seems to me that we are *all* on trial in the Eyes of Eternity.

When I went to record the Burial Dance only thirteen Luo Elders could be gathered together for a sum of three hundred shillings and I even had to collect some of you from Masogo, the headquarters of Chief Michael Kiyogo, in my Volkswagen – do you remember?

*Agnus Dei qui tollis peccata mundi:*
*miserere nobis*

'. . . I am now writing from Patrick Apoon's cousins' *manyatta* near the place of the Elephant Trees, using Patrick's pen and ink which makes things easier. Patrick, a student from Moroto Secondary School, has been helping me translate the songs of his relatives who live in the bush. His cousin is absolutely beautiful and is very pleased because I brought her tobacco, groundnuts, flour and sweets. She has many children but is still so young. She is naked to the waist and has become upset because the Priest has informed her that since she is now baptized she must cover herself up – but naturally she has full breasts and is very proud of them, having had many children which have helped to draw her breasts downwards so that they hang flatly on her chest. Patrick says this is a sign of being fruitful; he doesn't agree with the Priest and nor do I . . .'

*O Lamb of God, who takest away the sins of the world, have mercy on us*
'. . . Patrick's stepfather who owns cattle, sheep and goats, walks with the aid of a crutch, and when he extends his hard hand towards me and exchanges the greetings of Karamoja, he says:

> Mata! Mata!
> > I am greeting you because,
> Mata angakinae
> > of the goods you have,
> Mata anguatuk
> > because of cows,
> Mata angitunga
> > because of the people you have,
> Mata ngimwomwa
> > in the name of grain,
> Mata lore
> > in the name of the home,
> Mata nawui
> > I wish you a happy stay in the grazing area.

You do not say "Mata" with an Oxford accent, you accentuate the "ta" and grunt slightly. You do not look away when you are attracted to Patrick's cousin – you do not think "how odd", because you realize that Patrick is a miracle and that his grandmother, who is sitting behind me, being a very wise person, sold cows so that Patrick could go to school . . .'

*Tu solus Sanctus. Thou alone art Holy*
'. . . I first became aware of Alepir, one of Patrick's sisters, when we

195

returned from the wells at the Omaniman river. It was her shadow that first caught my attention and then the soft shuffling of her little bare feet in the pathway which the people use to come and go.

She walked very close behind me, never loosing a foot or gaining an inch. She moved in my path like a perfectly smooth fitting, gliding along the same path which her great-grandmothers used long ago.

I felt such a lump. No grace or skill – just a sort of BBC reporter with baggy trousers and a flappy bottom.

I kept turning round for sheer delight of seeing her little gliding self following behind and her big broad grin and white eyes underneath that huge, round, flat pot which she carried on her head all the way so smoothly. It was her job to fetch and carry water and she seemed to slip into my wake like a perfect holiday.

So I said to Patrick – and he replied:

"She's my little sister."

"Well what's her name?" I asked.

"Alepir," he replied.

So every time I looked around I said as if I were being slightly grown up –

"ALEPairrRRRR?"

And each time she rewarded me with a grin!

Patrick says she is about six "dry seasons" old and according to her generation she is named after a Mouse!

The children love to sing about "The Mouse" praising it and naming their friends after it. They sit and sway from side to side slapping their hands on their knees in a beautiful rhythm crying out:

> HOR-OOH, HOR-YEH-YA!
>     The rest of the mice cry when Lonang died.
>     (Solo)
> HOR-OOH, HOR-YEH-YA!
>     They have killed my friend and mice are crying.
> HOR-OOH, HOR-YEH-YA!
>     Mice cry for Lonang.

HOR-OOH, HOR-YEH-YA!
> They have killed my friend and the granaries
> are no longer with holes.

HOR-OOH, HOR-YEH-YA!
> They have killed my friend Napaekang.

HOR-OOH, HOR-YEH-YA!
> The rest of the mice cry when Lonang died.

Well, what about Education? We had been walking for a very long time – and we have been walking for a very long time *since* that time. During the night in Patrick Apoon's stepfather's *manyatta* as I drank goat's milk from a gourd given me by the one little Mouse and as I held her on my knee I said to Patrick – "She must go to school."

And there began a big question . . .'

*Agnus Dei, qui tollis peccata mundi:*
*miserere nobis*
'. . . Patrick said, as we said goodbye, a touching thing and I almost choked because of it – you see, *that* is travel and somehow each little adventure leaves behind a person without whose help the adventure would not have happened.

"Mr David, since the time that we have been together I too have learnt something. I have learnt what it is to want to learn something and how to do it – our meetings have been like jewels for they are priceless. One day I hope to see you in your homeland." . . .'

Patrick and I spent twelve days together recording and translating the songs of his family. Apart from thanking him I send greetings and hope that he did manage to get to Makerere University as he had hoped.

*Dona nobis pacem. Grant us peace*
'. . . It is a perfect evening – no wind and no discomfort of any kind. The sun is almost gone and a lamp sits on the table in front of our home. It is that sort of evening one wishes all one's life to come. In the gloom sits a man with a huge plume of feathers crowning his head. We have

just been for a long walk across the bush to a neighbouring village.

It's just like being in the theatre – my lamp is the footlight – beyond I see nothing; I just hear the noises of Africa and a girl stands right in front of me with her hands on her hips – she is five dry seasons old I think.

The light against the Elephant Trees makes a strange pattern in the sky.

Lomongin is crying again, she has been suffering from bad tummy-aches, so I have given her mother four pills to help her. The man with the crown of feathers has gone inside the *manyatta*.

I am expecting the moon to rise over Moroto Mountain at any moment.

It is all true – I can hardly believe it.

As we passed the place where the dancing was – I stopped. It was like a magic circle – just a smooth patch of mud, bone dry and worn down by years of 'Edonga' dance.

Do you think the Spirits saw me standing there? I just imagined fairies jumping like naughty puffed wheats shot from a gun!

I didn't see an elephant, I didn't kill a lion or step on a snake. I stopped and found it hard to remember the place because – when I am old, I shall forget a little of the enchantment.

When the moon rose over Moroto Mountain the clapping began and girls came from all the neighbouring districts singing songs of expectancy as they approached the jumping area.

In the moonlight the men formed circles and with sticks they held under their arms they challenged the girls, twisting their jumping bodies as high as the lower branches of the Elephant Trees. The girls jumped too with friends, quite little jumps, enough for the men to see them jumping. This went on for hours until the moon was high – then engagements took place.

Two men approach a girl. If she runs away, she is not interested. If she stands "looking", holding her chin up with her hand, "looking away", then she is "listening". The best friend of the man who wishes to be married proposes that his friend would like to engage her and that he has so many cows. If she accepts then the marriage is sealed about two months later and the cows become the property of the girl's father.

It was all going on last night, long after I wrapped myself up in a beautiful skin which we had been sitting on during the day.

I heard them clapping in my sleep.

Yesterday I went back to the school at the mission and had tea with the teachers. I saw many little "mice" eating their supper on the ground. They were all dressed alike.

Alepir was not there.

I felt moved because a part of me knew that these little mice had been "saved" and that in the care of education they were being given a different chance.

Like Patrick, they would never return to the bush – they would seek and find a new life.

And so I finish.

Now the very fact was, whether it actually was or wasn't made little difference because, when finally I *had* finished and returned to my bicycle which Patrick had lent me, I found it had a puncture!

So we walked the remaining twenty miles back to the Italian Fathers and arrived with a magnificent glow darkening over the far horizon . . .'

# XV

# *Gloria*

I have carved a Cross upon Africa.
That is what I have been doing.

Cairo represents the Crown of Thorns,
West and East Sudan represent the spread of
cultivation and peace.

The South represents the suffering,
Tribal differences and injustice.

The Lake represents the source of life.
It is the Earth giving water to the roots of a huge
    tree,
two thousand miles long.

This Tree bears *much* music and I have tried to
    find it.

Sometimes I have succeeded,
and other times I have failed.

But may God give us the Spirit for peace at this
    time
and a Happy Christmas.

# *Coda*

'Mr David, why did you do it?' asked the Hippo Man after a long and appreciative silence. 'Why did you make the Sanctus Journey?'

'I did it, your Courtship, because I felt I needed to do it. Because I knew you would understand – after all when you dance in Africa you like competition, many groups performing all at the same time.'

'True, true, that is very true indeed,' said the Hippo Man.

'I did it because I wanted to celebrate the changing mood of music today, for we are all living and sharing life together on a very small planet, your Courtship.'

'Very true, that is very true indeed,' replied the Hippo Man. 'We have been seeing many tourists recently and we are proud and like to praise them. Are you a tourist Mr David?'

'No, not quite, your Courtship. I am a composer and a traveller and I have a lot of people to thank for making my travels possible – governments, district officers, missionaries, headmasters, students and of course, the musicians and dancers themselves. Without hearing their music my ambition and my creativity would never be fulfilled.'

'True, true.' The Hippo Man then turned to all the other Witch Doctors, Elders, Members of the Jury and Greater Public who were by this time whispering in hushed tones of contentment.

'This is only the beginning,' continued the Defendant, 'but before I go on I would like the Court to hear the advice of a Mzee* who has perhaps influenced my thinking more than I fully appreciate. This particular Mzee is quite an old hand at giving important advice and I would, therefore, like to call upon The Father.'

'We call upon The Father . . . er . . . Colonel Fanshawe to give us advice,' said the Hippo Man. Is Colonel present?'

* A very wise and respected Elder.

The Father, wearing the suit he usually wears on Sunday mornings, came up the aisle of the Courtroom as if he were about to read the Epistle from the New Translation of the Bible in Bilsington Church. Having entered the witness box, under the lower branches of the Elephant Tree, he adjusted his glasses and read out very clearly what he had so carefully prepared to deliver after breakfast. The Father is a very methodical reader who says:

'A battle is won by pockets of men who occupy little pockets of isolated territory they care nothing about. When, in the face of the enemy, every instinct tells them to run, to get the hell out of it, a battle is won by the man in the pocket who can hold out that little bit longer against every instinct he's got. It's the same principle in Industry and it's the same with Music. Success and victory are achieved by the man who can hold his ground.

'Therefore I say, hold *your* ground; and the other thing I say to you is this – 2% of people DO and 98% of people wish they had. Very few people achieve their aims, the vast majority look back and say "OH! if *only* I had . . ." '

'Thank you Colonel,' said the Hippo Man, 'there is just one question I would like to ask – do you spell your name Featherstonhaugh?'

'No, M'Lud, I spell my name Fanshawe and as far as I am aware there are no Fanshawes who spell their name in any other way.'

'Thank you, Colonel, for your advice and I hope in return *we* shall have the pleasure of visiting you in your bit of isolated territory some day.' The Hippo Man then asked Members of the Jury if they had come to a decision.

'We have, M'Lud,' replied the Jury.

'Then what is your decision? Have you reached your verdict and is it the verdict of you all? Is the Defendant Guilty or Not Guilty in the Eyes of Eternity?'

The Defendant, swaying from side to side, gazed out of the window at the tennis court upon the hill and repeated the Secret:

'PUMP, what lies beyond the Hills?'

'Guilty or Not Guilty in the Eyes of Eternity?' said the Hippo Man.

## Coda

'There's been some disagreement M'Lud' replied the Chief of the Court and the Municipal Armory, not knowing quite what to say next.

But in the distance, far away, the people in the courtroom were heard to be softly singing:

'FIRST THE LAND and THEN THE SEA, FIRST THE LAND and THEN THE SEA, FIRST THE LAND and THEN THE SEA . . .'

Forever and
> forever and
>> forever.

# Ultimate Cure

I know what I am,
You know what You are,
They know what?
He knows what He is,
She knows what She is,
But some of us are more like Potatoes than others.

This book is, therefore, a Potato,
If it were not,
It would all be lies.

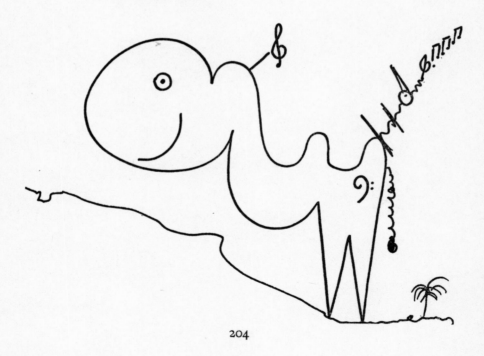

# Postscript

When the Committee of the Ralph Vaughan Williams Trust heard of David Fanshawe's plan to travel down the Nile to collect and record the music native to the countries in those still remote areas, we were both interested and impressed by his project. We knew how quickly the spreading and greedy tentacles of modern technological power can damage, if not ruin, old and traditional patterns of life and the culture that belongs to such lives. We knew, too, from the examples of collectors of folk music working at the beginning of this century, what musical treasures have been rescued from oblivion in our own islands, in America – from the descendants of the early settlers and from Europe, where musicians of the stature of Bartók and Kodály devoted much time to this work. So we were glad to be able to help with some of the expenses for David Fanshawe's expedition, having been assured of his musical ability and his technical control of the means by which he would record what music he could discover. In the early days of folk song collecting, musicians had to rely on taking down both words and music in their notebooks or on the clumsy, heavy, and unreliable phonographs, when singers had to be interrupted while the roll was changed, for besides all the other disadvantages, the music-rolls were very short, and singers often found it impossible to go on from where their song had been broken off. So most of the work done by such collectors as Cecil Sharp, Ralph Vaughan Williams, George Butterworth and Percy Grainger depended on their own knowledge, experience and care, and the actual voice of the singers – shepherds, sailors, workmen, farm labourers, poachers, girls and their grandmothers – have been lost, although the songs, which they had inherited, were saved for us all. Now, with the delicate portable machinery available, the actual sound of the voices of the singers and speakers can be preserved as well as the transcribed music which they sing.

David Fanshawe set off on his journey equipped to record and to photograph, and equipped by temperament to take advantage of whatever adventures this treasure-hunt might offer.

One of the hazards of such a journey is, of course, the loneliness that is inevitable for some part of the time when lack of a common language leaves the traveller outside the life around him. These hours provided time for letter writing and David Fanshawe kept us in touch with his life, sending a series of long letters to the Trust. His adventures on that first journey were funny, sad, strange, full of fortunate coincidences and maddening bad luck, which, by the time the next instalment reached us, had turned out to be good luck, after all. It was a lively and picturesque chronicle. It seemed that our traveller had made good use of his time, both in collecting original material and finding inspiration for his own work as a composer. The trophies of this journey and his later ones have not robbed the people from whom they are won, but enriched them, and show us wider landscapes than those we had known before.

*Ursula Vaughan Williams*

*February 28th 1974.*

## L'Envoi

Grandpa (96!) died peacefully and was buried in Farnham Parish churchyard next to his wife, Granny Mosse, during the fifth rewrite of the First Epistle according to Fanshawe. His funeral took place on the afternoon of 11 July, 1974.

Judith gave birth to Alexander David Fanshawe on 24 October 1974 at Queen Mary's Hospital, Roehampton.

# Acknowledgements

First and foremost I should like to thank my wife Judith, for her invaluable strength and support in preparing at least *five* typescripts of this Epistle – a thankless task on top of pregnancy!

Secondly Mrs George Villiers and Ernestine Novak for their editorial skills and encouragement at Harvill Press.

Thirdly Sir Keith Falkner and Mrs Ursula Vaughan Williams for writing the Foreword and Postscript.

A special thanks to Chappell & Co. Ltd, for kind permission to quote music illustrations, to Phonogram International, to Visual Publications for permission to reproduce the Date Picker, to the Executors of the Estate of Harold Owen, Chatto & Windus Ltd and New Directions Publishing Corporation for permission to quote from Wilfred Owen's poem 'The Parable of the Old Man and the Young', to Kafetz Cameras Ltd and A.V. Distributors (London) for photographic and sound equipment expertise.

In debt and deeply overdrawn greetings to Mr Palmer at Lloyds Bank, Hythe.

Grateful appreciation to the R.V.W. Trust, the Winston Churchill Memorial Trust for sponsorship; to the British Council and the Arts Council of Great Britain, also to Mrs Margaret Clouston, Miss Williams and The Mouse for lending original letters.

Many thanks to the following who have rescued, advised and assisted me in all matters including spelling – Lawrence de Souza, M.B.E., John Inglis Hall, John Lambert, Geoffrey Hancock, Herbert Chappell, Michael McCarthy, Keith Desmond, Dennis Stokes, Tom and Joan Fanshawe, James Fanshawe, St George's School, Stowe, the Royal College of Music, Jeremy Hunter, Baroness Guirne van Zuylen,

John Aspinwall, John Eames, Major and Mrs V. E. Kirkland, Ross Stainton, Richard Muir, Peter Johnson, Teddy Holmes, Erik Smith, Ernst van der Vossen, Dr Michael Cox, Anthony Friese-Greene, Mr and Mrs Oliver Brooke, Clare Pollen, Ken and Anna Gourlay, Penny Grant, Alice Brown, Sally Dickson, John Peacock, Sandra Mason (legal advisor!), John Weatherby, the Mother-in-Law – Mrs Paula Grant – and Mrs Gwen Streets, M. B. E.

Further appreciation and grateful thanks to Government Departments for permission to carry out musical research in Iraq, Kuwait, Bahrain, Abu Dhabi, Egypt, Sudan, Uganda, and Kenya and to the Missionaries of all denominations who helped 'in the field' – to teachers, guides, especially Basil Ali Hateem, Khalifah Shaheen, Emile Azer Wahba, Shaikh Mohammed el Amin Tirik, John Matura, Saleh Adam Gasim, Charles Krop, Patrick Apoon, Daniel Awuor, John Matarupash Meritey, educational authorities, all critics, not forgetting Truck Drivers!

I would also like to mention the British Army, Royal Navy and Royal Air Force, to thank them for their assistance, as well as B.A.P.C.O., Bahrain.

Finally my special thanks to Them at Home for supplying black and white pictures and for putting up with an awful lot; to the Map of Africa and *Winnie-the-Pooh*, all Potato growers and pickers and the Guardian Angel who gets me home in one piece. I hope no one is left out!

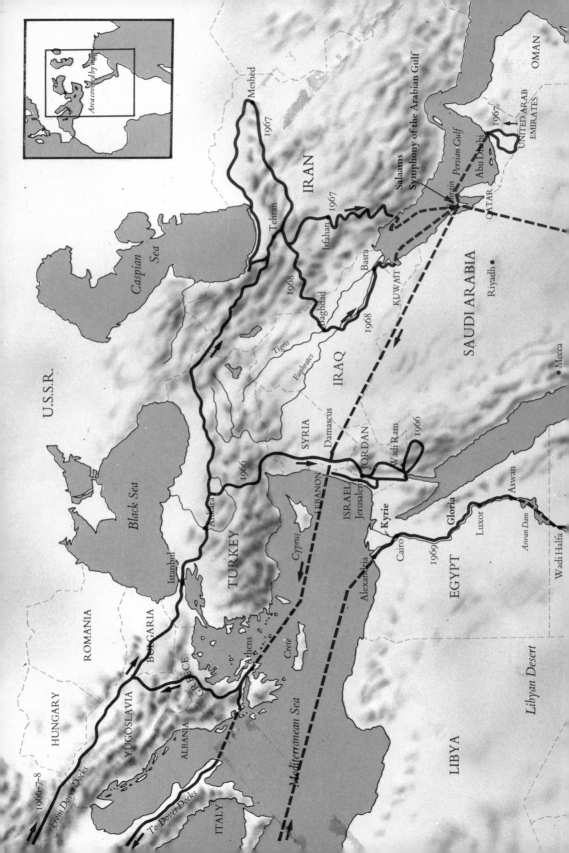